Crochet Patterns

GNOMES
Flowers & Garden Edition

Dear Crocheter,

I am thrilled to introduce this crochet book. As an avid crocheter, I wanted to create something that was not only fun to make but also brought joy and a sense of magic to our everyday lives. Crafting your own garden gnome can add a touch of whimsy to your outdoor (and indoor) space, and I hope that these patterns will inspire you to create your own unique and charismatic gnome characters.

I want to express my deepest gratitude for your support and interest in my book. Creating these patterns has been a journey of passion and perseverance, and I am excited to share it with you. I hope that you enjoy the patterns and have fun creating your own garden gnomes!

With each pattern, I encourage you to experiment with different colors and accessories to truly make each garden gnome your own. The possibilities are endless, and I hope that these patterns will spark your imagination and creativity.

I couldn't have done this alone and I'd like to thank my amazing team for their help and support. I am grateful for the support of my talented pattern tester, Elaine Lee, who tirelessly tested every pattern and provided invaluable feedback. Galina, my mom and video maker, deserves a special thanks for her informative videos that will guide you through the patterns, as well as for her stunning garden, which was a limitless source of inspiration for me. And last but not least, I would like to express my gratitude to Olga Kudrjavceva, whose corrections and invaluable feedback helped shape this book.

I hope that you enjoy the patterns and have fun creating your garden gnomes!

Happy crocheting!

Sincerely, Maria Ermolova

Page 21

Page 29

Page 57

Page 49

Page 65

Page 111

Page 101

Page 93

Page 143

Page 73

Page 137

Page 121

Page 129

Page 39

Page 85

Recommendations

NOTE: The yarn and tools stated in this section are suitable for all projects from this book.

Yarn

Blend: cotton and acrylic fiber yarn
Yarn Weight: Sport / Fine
Yarn length/weight: approx. 160 meters (174 yds) per 50 gram ball.
Yarn ideas: YarnArt Jeans(used for designs from this book), Scheepjes Softfun, Sirdar Snuggly Replay DK

If you are going to use different from the required yarn, you need to grab a crochet hook that suitable for your yarn and gauge/tension should be tight enough, so the toy stuffing doesn't show up through the crocheted fabric.

Tools

Crochet Hook in Metric Size Range: 2.5 mm
Stitch markers x2

Gauge/Tension

Rd 1	6SC in magic ring, tighten the ring [6]
Rd 2	INC in each st around [12]
Rd 3	*(SC in next st, INC in next st)from*rep x6 [18]
Rd 4	*(SC in next st, INC in next st, SC in next st) from*rep x6 [24]
Rd 5	*(SC in next 3 sts, INC in next st) from*rep x6 [30]
Rd 6	*(SC in next 2 sts, INC in next st, SC in next 2ˢᵗs) from*rep x6 [36]

Size: Ø 4.5-5 cm
When using yarn that is different from the required type, it's important to keep in mind that your crocheted fabric should be tight enough to prevent fillers from showing through the stitches.

Recommendations

Tips Before You Start

Single Crochet "V" and "X"
The typical method to make a single crochet is to insert your hook into a stitch, yarn over, pull through, yarn over, pull through both loops. This method makes a 'V' stitch.
The other lesser-known method to make a single crochet is to insert your hook into a stitch, yarn under, pull through, yarn over, pull through both loops. This method makes an 'X' stitch.
Please, note that I use SC "x".

Scan for the video tutorial

Lifehack

You can use these crocheted gnomes as a door stop.
Make a small fabric bag (a size 10 cm x 15 cm or so) (as well you can use a finished small pouch bag and stitch along an opening when a bag is filled with some filler)
Fill with Pebbles, cat litter, washed sand, rice or beans (food may attract insects)
After completing the first round of decreases at the bottom of the gnome's body, you can insert the bag containing the filler and and the rest of the filler.
Then, resume crocheting to complete the project.

Abbreviations (US terms)

Scan for the video tutorial

St(s)	Stitch/es
Rd	Round
Ch	Chain stitch
SC	Single Crochet "X"
DC	Double Crochet: yarn over, insert hook in stitch, yarn over, pull through stitch, [yarn over, pull through two loops] twice
sl st	slip stitch: insert hook in stitch, yarn over, pull through both loops on hook
hdc	Half Double Crochet: yarn over, insert in stitch, yarn over, pull through st, yarn over, pull through all 3 loops on hook
TR	Triple crochet: Yarn over the hook 2 times and insert your hook in indicated stitch. Yarn over the hook and pull hook through stitch. Yarn over the hook and draw your yarn through the first 2 loops on your hook. Yarn over the hook and draw your yarn through the next 2 loops on your hook. Yarn over the hook and draw your yarn through the last 2 loops on your hook.
SC2tog	Single crochet two together: Insert hook into stitch and draw up a loop. Insert hook into next stitch and draw up a loop. Yarn over, draw through all 3 loops on hook.
SC2tog_inv	Single crochet two stitches together invisible decrease: insert your hook into a next front loop, then insert a hook in next front loop, yarn over and draw through 2 loops on a hook. Then yarn over again and draw through 2 loops on a hook.
INC	Increase: single crochet in one stitch twice
Ch-space	Chain-space
prev	previous

Abbreviations (US terms)

BLO	Back loop only
FLO	Front Loop only
*(_) from*rep x	work instructions within parentheses as many times as directed by x
Surface slip stitch	Place a thread behind the fabric, insert hook into the crocheted fabric from the front to the back and grab yarn on hook, pull a loop through to the front. Insert hook from front to back and pull a loop to the front side and through the loop on the front of the fabric to create a surface slipped stitch. Begin by placing your yarn behind the fabric(in case, your fabric has a wrong side). Your working yarn will remain on the underside of your work while you surface crochet. Insert a hook into the fabric from the front to the back, and pull a loop through to the front. Insert hook from front to back and pull a loop to the front side and through the loop on the front of the fabric to create a surface slipped stitch.
Bobble st	Work 4 unfinished double crochet in one stitch and complete them all together (for a detailed photo tutorial, please refer to page 40 and watch a video tutorial)
BPhdc	Back post half double crochet (back post - see below)
FPsc	Front post single crochet
INVISIBLE FINISH FOR OPEN CROCHET EDGES	MAGIC RING
FP/BP	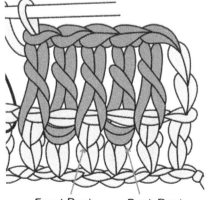

Front Post   Back Post

Photo Tutorial - Leaf

1) **Light Green:** Foundation chain: Chain 8

2) sl st in 2nd st from hook, sl st in next 6 sts, Ch1,

3) Work in bottom of a foundation chain: SC in next st,

4) hdc in next st,

5) 2DC in each of next 2sts,

6) hdc in next st,

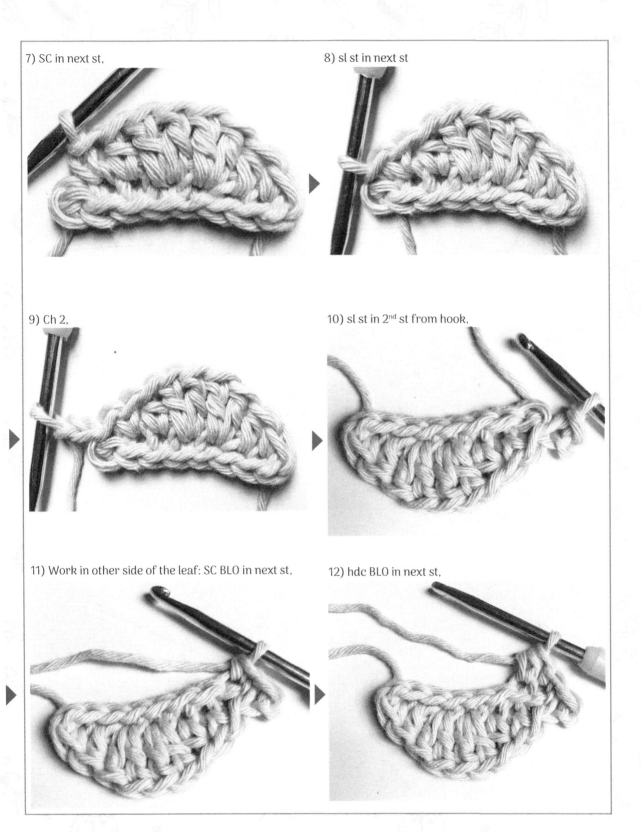

7) SC in next st,

8) sl st in next st

9) Ch 2,

10) sl st in 2nd st from hook,

11) Work in other side of the leaf: SC BLO in next st,

12) hdc BLO in next st,

13) DC BLO in next 2 sts, hdc BLO in next st,

14) SC BLO in next st,

15) sl st BLO in next st. The first leaf is completed.

16) Ch8,

17) Sl st in 2nd st from hook, sl st in next 6sts, Ch 1

18) SC in next st on other side of a chain,

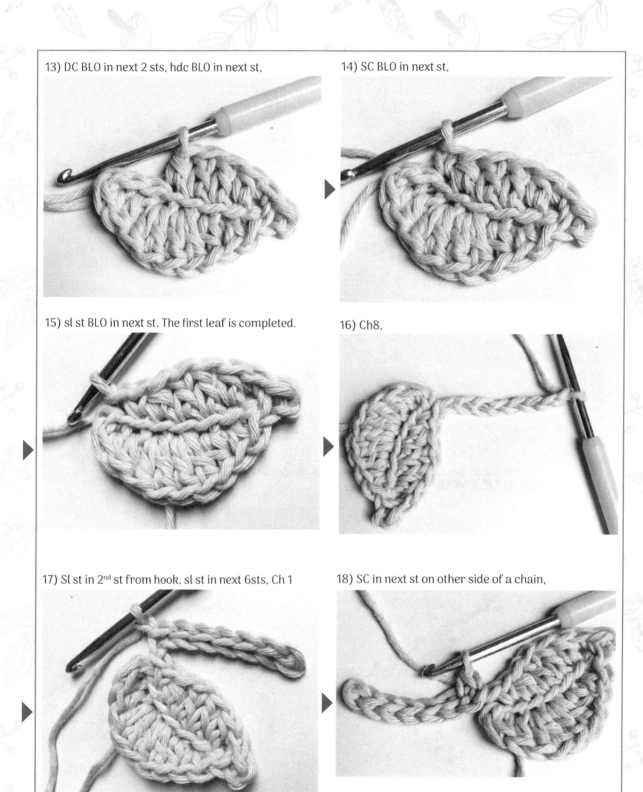

19) hdc in next st, 2DC in each of next 2 sts, hdc in next st, SC in next st, sl st in next st, Ch2,

20) Sl st in 2nd st from hook, SC BLO in next st in other side of the chain, hdc BLO in next st, DC BLO in next 2sts, hdc BLO in next st, SC BLO in next st, sl st BLO in next st. The second leaf is completed.

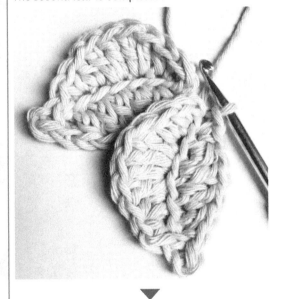

21) Ch8, Turn

22) Sl st in 2nd st from hook, sl st in next 6sts,

23) Ch 1, SC in next st on other side of the chain, hdc in next st, 2DC in each of next 2 sts, hdc in next st, SC in next st, sl st in next st, Ch2, Turn

24) sl st in 2nd st from hook, SC BLO in next st, hdc BLO in next st, DC BLO in next 2 sts, hdc BLO in next st, SC BLO in next st, sl st in next st

HOW TO - Color changing

You need to follow the pattern until it is time to switch colors, in the stitch previous to the new color, complete the final yarn over and draw through with the new color you are switching to.

Always change color in the last stitch of a current color completing the last stitch with a new color.

Chamomile

1) Foundation chain: Chain 7

2) sl st in the first chain stitch of the foundation chain

3) **Chain 5

4) hdc in 3rd st from hook

5) hdc in each of next st

6) SC in next st,

7) Sl st in next st of the foundation chain

Repeat steps from (**) x7 more times (8 petals)

DISC

Rd 1   6SC in magic ring, tighten the ring

Rd 2   *(SC in next st, INC in next st)from*rep x3 [9]

Rd 3   SC in each st around [9]

Sew the disc on the petal part in the middle

Small Rose

Chain 19

Row 1   3DC in 3rd st from hook, sl st in next st, *(Ch1, 3DC in next st, sl st in next st) from*rep to end

Roll it up tightly, shaping the rose, and sew it at the bottom, making sure to thread through all the layers to ensure a secure hold

Large Rose

Chain 20

Row 1   SC in 2nd st from hook, SC in next 18 sts [19] Turn

Row 2   skip next st, *(Ch1, 4DC in next st, Ch1, sl st in next st) from*rep x9 [9 petals]

Roll it up tightly, shaping the rose, and sew it at the bottom, making sure to thread through all the layers to ensure a secure hold

How to - Twisted Cord

To create your desired final cord length, it's important to start with a thread length that is three times longer. For instance, if you want your cord to be around 50 cm long, you'll need to grab threads that are approximately 150 cm each.

1. Choose the necessary colors and grab at least 2 threads
2. Once you have your threads, tie a knot on one end and hook it onto something sturdy, like a door handleFold in half and remove the end from the door handle.
3. Start to twist the threads together, making sure to twist them well.
4. Once you've achieved a good twist, fold the threads in half and remove the end from the door handle holding both ends.
5. Straighten the cord and make a knot on the other end

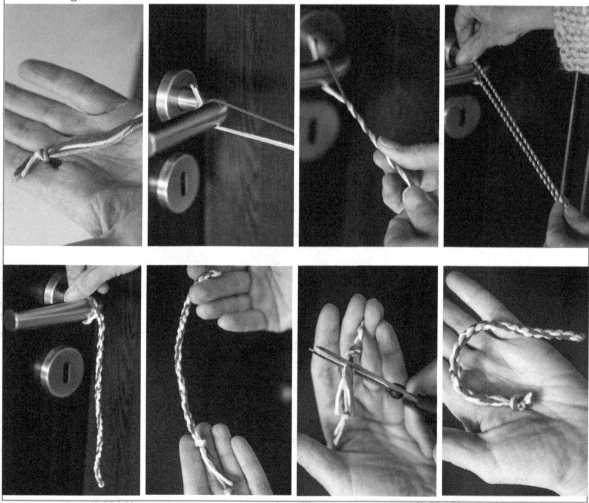

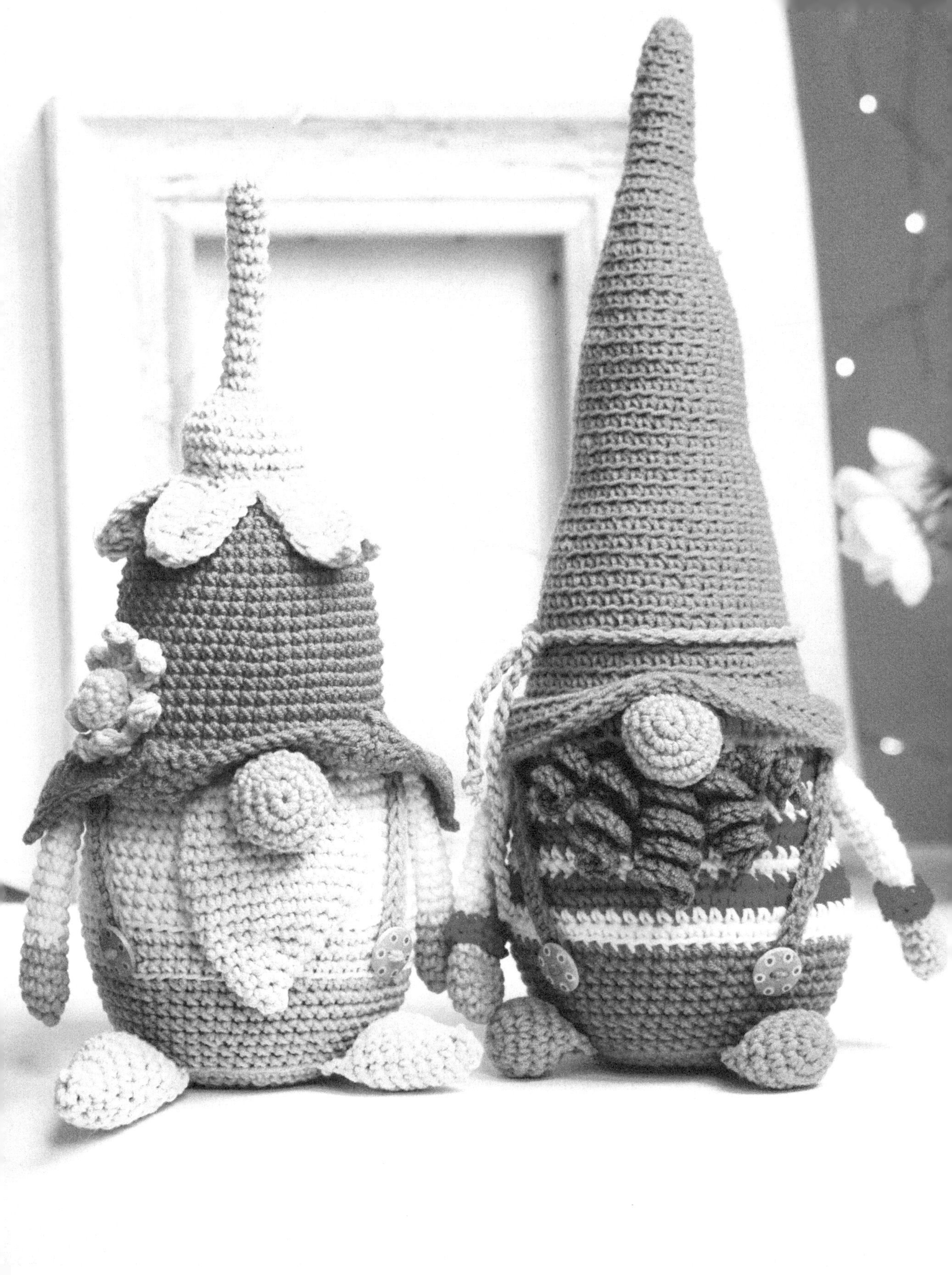

Lady Gardener

SIZE: 26 cm / 10 in

YARN BRAND AND COLORS			TOTAL FOR A PROJECT
Mustard	★	Yarn Art Jeans 84	Approx. 20 g/70 meters
Off-White	☆	Yarn Art Jeans 03	Approx. 10 g/35 meters
Honey caramel	★	Yarn Art Jeans 07	Approx. 7 g/25 meters
Jeans Blue	★	Yarn Art Jeans 68	Approx. 25 g/90 meters
Brown	★	Yarn Art Jeans 40	Approx. 10 g/35 meters
Red	★	Yarn Art Jeans 90	Approx. 2 g
Grass Green	★	Yarn Art Jeans 69	Approx. 2 g

OTHER MATERIALS	CROCHET STICHES	TOOLS
Stuffing approx. 40 g	St(s), Ch, hdc, SC, INC, DC, sl st, SC2tog, BLO, FLO, surface slip stitch	Crochet Hook 2.5 mm Tapestry needle

Make sure to use a contrasting thread to clearly mark the beginning of each round of your project. Don't remove the thread until your work is completed.

STEP 1. HEAD+BODY (work in continuous rounds)

Rd 1	**Mustard:** 6SC in magic ring [6] tighten the ring
Rd 2	INC in each st around [12]
Rd 3	*(SC in next st, INC in next st)from*rep x6 [18]
Rd 4	*(SC in next st, INC in next st, SC in next st)from*rep x6 [24]
Rd 5	*(SC BLO in next 3sts, INC BLO in next st)from*rep x6 [30]
Rd 6	*(SC BLO in next 2sts, INC BLO in next st, SC BLO in next 2sts)from*rep x6 [36]
Rd 7	*(SC BLO in next 5sts, INC BLO in next st)from*rep x6 [42]
Rd 8	*(SC BLO in next 3sts, INC BLO in next st, SC BLO in next 3sts)from*rep x6 [48]
Rd 9	*(SC BLO in next 7sts, INC BLO in next st)from*rep x6 [54]
Rd 10	*(SC BLO in next 4sts, INC BLO in next st, SC BLO in next 4sts)from*rep x6 [60]
Rd 11-21	SC BLO in each st around [60] Change to **Off-White** in last st. Cut off **Mustard**

Place a stitch marker into last st of Rd 21. This will serve as a guide for later when we crochet the brim.

Rd 22	**Off-White:** SC BLO in each st around [60]
Rd 23	SC in next 14sts, SC BLO in next 10sts(the arm and braid will be attached to these stitches), SC in next 4sts, SC BLO in next 4sts (the nose will be attached to these stitches), SC in next 4sts, SC BLO in next 10sts(the arm and braid will be attached to these stitches), SC in next 14sts [60]
Rd 22-30	SC in each st around [60] Change to **Jeans Blue** in last st. Cut off **Off-White**
Rd 31	**Jeans Blue:** SC BLO in each st around [60]
	Note: we will attach a skirt to these stitches FLO later
Rd 32-38	SC in each st around [60]
Rd 39	*(SC in next 13sts, SC2tog)from*rep x4 [56]
Rd 40-41	SC in each st around [56]
Rd 42	*(SC in next 6sts, SC2tog, SC in next 6sts)from*rep x4 [52]
Rd 43-44	SC in each st around [52]

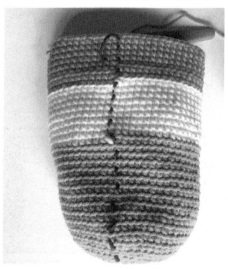

| Rd 45 | *(SC in next 11sts, SC2tog)from*rep x4 [48] |
| Rd 46 | SC BLO in each st around [48] |

Note: we will attach shoes to these stitches FLO later

| Rd 47 | *(SC in next 2sts, SC2tog, SC in next 2sts)from*rep x8 [40] |

Stuff

Rd 48	*(SC in next 3sts, SC2tog)from*rep x8 [32]
Rd 49	*(SC in next st, SC2tog, SC in next st)from*rep x8 [24]
Rd 50	*(SC in next st, SC2tog)from*rep x8 [16]

Stuff

| Rd 51 | SC2tog x8 [8] |

Cut off a thread and sew the opening, weave in

STEP 2. HAT BRIM (work in continuous rounds)

Rd 1	**Mustard:** Grab the body upside-down. Work into stitches FLO of Rd 21, start from the stitch marker: *(SC FLO in next 7sts, INC FLO in next st, SC FLO in next 7sts)from*rep x4 [64]
Rd 2	*(SC BLO in next 15sts, INC BLO in next)from*rep x4 [68]
Rd 3	*(SC BLO in next 8sts, INC BLO in next, SC BLO in next 8sts)from*rep x4 [72]
Rd 4	*(SC BLO in next 17sts, INC BLO in next)from*rep x4 [76]
Rd 5	sl st in each st around [76]

Cut off **Mustard** and weave in

Jeans Blue: work surface slip stitches into stitches of Rd 21 of the hat (start from the beginning of rd)

Red: work surface slip stitches into stitches of Rd 20 of the hat (start from the beginning of rd)

Cut off threads and weave in ends

STEP 3. NOSE (work in continuous rounds)

Rd 1	**Honey caramel:** 6SC in magic ring [6] tighten the ring
Rd 2	INC in each st around [12]
Rd 3	*(SC in next st, INC in next st)from*rep x6 [18]
Rd 4-5	SC in each st around [18]
Rd 6	*(SC in next st, SC2tog)from*rep x6 [12]

Cut off a thread, leaving a long tail for sewing. Stuff the nose with a small amount of stuffing

Attach the nose by sewing or gluing it onto the front of the body, to 4 stitches FLO under the hat brim.

STEP 4. BRAIDS
(make 6 sections (3 for each of 2 braids))

| | **Brown:** Chain 30 |
| Row 1 | DC in 4th st from hook, DC in next 26 sts [28] |

Cut off a thread, leave a long tail for sewing Once you have completed the three sections, stitch them together as shown in picture. Once that is complete, weave in the ends of the yarn, leaving just one for sewing.

Once the nose attachment is complete, you will need to attach each braid to the stitches FLO under the hat brim on the side next to the arm as shown in pictures below (in between the arm and nose). Do the braid and tie off with a **Red** yarn.

ARMs (make x2) (work in continuous rounds)

STEP 1. ARM

Rd 1	**Honey caramel:** 5SC in magic ring [5] tighten the ring
Rd 2	INC in each st around [10]
Rd 3-5	SC in each st around [10] Change to **Off-White** in last st. Cut off **Honey caramel**
Rd 6	**Off-White:** SC in each st around [10]
Rd 7	SC BLO in each st around [10]
Rd 8-17	SC in each st around [10]

Cut off **Off-White**, leave a long tail for sewing

STEP 2. CUFF

Rd 1	Hold the arm upside-down and with **Red** work into stitches FLO Rd 6: SC FLO in each st around [10]

Cut off **Red** and weave in

To attach the arms, sew them onto the sides of the body under the hat brim using the available stitches FLO. You have 10 stitches available on each side for attaching the arms and braids. Be sure to attach the arms in such a way that the stitches in front are left available for attaching the braids

SHOES (make x2) (work in continuous rounds)

Rd 1	**Mustard:** 6SC in magic ring [6] tighten the ring
Rd 2	INC in each st around [12]
Rd 3	*(SC in next st, INC in next st) from*rep x6 [18]
Rd 4-6	SC in each st around [18]
Rd 7	*(SC in next st, SC2tog) from*rep x6 [12]

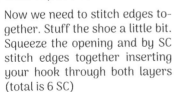

Now we need to stitch edges together. Stuff the shoe a little bit. Squeeze the opening and by SC stitch edges together inserting your hook through both layers (total is 6 SC)

Cut off a thread, leave a long tail for sewing

Once you have finished attaching the skirt, proceed to attach the shoes onto the body using stitches on FLO of Round 45

SKIRT (work in rows)

	Jeans Blue: Chain 9 [9]
Row 1	SC in 2nd chain from hook, SC in next 7 sts [8] Ch1, Turn
Row 2-90	SC BLO in next 8sts, Ch1 [8] Turn
Row 91	Continue working into the side edge(a long edge - waistband): *(SC in each on next 2 rows, skip next row)from*rep x 30 [60]

Cut off thread, leave a long tail for sewing.
Sew on the stitches FLO of Rd 30 (stitch to stitch) of the body.

Crochet Flowers

Chamomile page 15

×1 **Off-White + Mustard**;

×1 **Jeans Blue + Mustard**

Small Rose – page 17

×1 **Red** – page 17

Leaves – page 10

× 1 **Green grass**

Attach flowers and leaves to the hat using either a sewing or glue method.

Gardener

SIZE: 30 cm / 11.8 in

YARN BRAND AND COLORs			TOTAL FOR A PROJECT
Mustard	★	Yarn Art Jeans 84	Approx. 15g/50 meters
Off-White	☆	Yarn Art Jeans 03	Approx. 10g /35 meters
Honey caramel	★	Yarn Art Jeans 07	Approx. 7g/25 meters
Jeans Blue	★	Yarn Art Jeans 68	Approx. 15g/50meter
Red	★	Yarn Art Jeans 90	Approx. 10g/35 meters
Brown	★	Yarn Art Jeans 40	Approx. 10g/35 meters
Light Grey	★	Yarn Art Jeans 46	Approx. 4 g/10 meters
Grass Green	★	Yarn Art Jeans 69	Approx. 2g

OTHER MATERIALS	CROCHET STICHES	TOOLS
Stuffing approx. 50g Decorative buttons Ø12mm x2 Dowel Rods Wood Sticks (1/8inch or 3mm) for Crafts	St(s), Ch, SC, DC, INC, sl st, SC2tog, BLO, FLO	Crochet hook 2.5 mm Tapestry needle

Note: Make sure to use a contrasting thread to clearly mark the beginning of each round of your project. Don't remove the thread until your work is completed.

Note: if cutting the yarn is not mentioned in the pattern, simply drop the yarn and pick it up again when needed

STEP 1. HAT + BODY (work in continuous rounds)

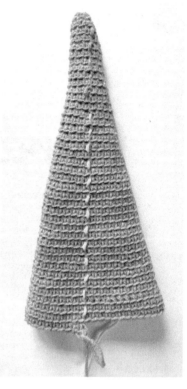

Rd 1	**Mustard:** 6SC in magic ring [6]tighten the ring
	For all stitches until Round 41, work them BLO.
Rd 2	SC in each st around [6]
Rd 3	*(INC in next st, SC in next st)from*rep x3[9]
Rd 4-5	SC in each st around [9]
Rd 6	*(SC in next st, INC in next st, SC in next st) from*rep x3 [12]
Rd 7-8	SC in each st around [12]
Rd 9	*(SC in next 3sts, INC in next st)from*rep x3 [15]
Rd 10-11	SC in each st around [15]
Rd 12	*(SC in next 2sts, INC in next st, SC in next 2sts) from*rep x3 [18]
Rd 13-14	SC in each st around [18]
Rd 15	*(SC in next 5sts, INC in next st)from*rep x3 [21]
Rd 16-17	SC in each st around [21]
Rd 18	*(SC in next 3sts, INC in next st, SC in next 3sts) from*rep x3 [24]
Rd 19-20	SC in each st around [24]
Rd 21	*(SC in next 7sts, INC in next st)from*rep x3 [27]
Rd 22-23	SC in each st around [27]
Rd 24	*(SC in next 4sts, INC in next st, SC in next 4sts) from*rep x3 [30]
Rd 25-26	SC in each st around [30]
Rd 27	*(SC in next 9sts, INC in next st)from*rep x3 [33]
Rd 28-29	SC in each st around [33]
Rd 30	*(SC in next 5sts, INC in next st, SC in next 5sts) from*rep x3 [36]
Rd 31-32	SC in each st around [36]
Rd 33	*(SC in next 11sts, INC in next st)from*rep x3 [39]
Rd 34-35	SC in each st around [39]
Rd 36	*(SC in next 6sts, INC in next st, SC in next 6sts) from*rep x3 [42]
Rd 37-38	SC in each st around [42]
Rd 39	*(SC in next 3sts, INC in next st, SC in next 3sts) from*rep **x6** [48]

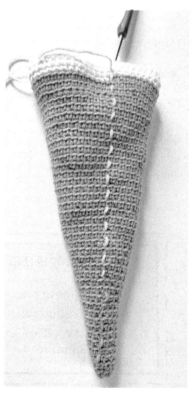

Rd 40-41	SC in each st around [48] Change to **Off-White** in last st. Cut off **Mustard**
Rd 42	**Off-White:** SC BLO in each st around [48]
Rd 43	SC in next 20sts, SC BLO in next 8sts (the beard will be attached to these sts), SC in next 20sts [48] Change to **Red** in last st.
Rd 44	**Red:** SC in each st around [48]
Rd 45	SC in next 9sts, SC BLO in next 6sts (the arm and strap will be attached to these sts), SC in next 18sts, SC BLO in next 6sts (the arm and strap will be attached to these sts), SC in next 9sts [48]. Change to **Off-White** in last st
Rd 46-47	**Off-White:** SC in each st around [48] Change to **Red** in last st
Rd 48	**Red:** SC in each st around [48]
Rd 49	*(SC in next 7sts, INC in next st)from*rep x6 [54]. Change to **Off-White** in last st
Rd 50-51	**Off-White:** SC in each st around [54] Change to **Red** in last st
Rd 52	**Red:** *(SC in next 4sts, INC in next st, SC in next 4sts) from*rep x6 [60]
Rd 53	SC in each st around [60] Change to **Off-White** in last st. Cut off **Red**
Rd 54	**Off-White:** *(SC in next 7sts, INC in next st, SC in next 7sts) from*rep **x4** [64]
Rd 55	SC in each st around [64] Change to **Jeans Blue** in last st. Cut off **Off-White**
Rd 56	**Jeans Blue:** SC BLO in each st around [64]
Rd 57	SC in each st around [64]
Rd 58	*(SC in next 3sts, SC2tog, SC in next 3sts) from*rep x8 [56]
Rd 59-60	SC in each st around [56]
Rd 61	*(SC in next 5sts, SC2tog)from*rep x8 [48]
	Stuff
Rd 62-63	SC in each st around [48]
Rd 64	SC BLO in each st around [48]
	Note: we will sew boots to these stitches FLO later
Rd 65	*(SC in next 2sts, SC2tog, SC in next 2sts)from*rep x8 [40]
Rd 66	*(SC in next 3sts, SC2tog)from*rep x8 [32]
Rd 67	*(SC in next st, SC2tog, SC in next st)from*rep x8 [24]
Rd 68	*(SC in next st, SC2tog)from*rep x8 [16]
	Stuff
Rd 69	SC2tog x8 [8]
	Cut off a thread and sew the opening, weave in

STEP 2. Continue - HAT BRIM
(work in continuous rounds)

Rd 1	Hold the piece upside-down. Join **Mustard** to the beginning of the rd 41 (the last **Mustard** round of the hat) and work into stitches FLO: *(SC FLO in next 7sts, INC FLO in next st) from*rep x6 [54]
Rd 2	*(SC BLO in next 4sts, INC BLO in next st, SC BLO in next 4sts) from*rep x6 [60]
Rd 3	*(SC BLO in next 9sts, INC BLO in next st) from*rep x6 [66]
Rd 4	*(SC BLO in next 5sts, INC BLO in next st, SC BLO in next 5sts) from*rep x6 [72]
Rd 5	sl st in each st around [72]

Cut off a thread. Weave in

ARMs (work in continuous rounds)

STEP 1. ARM

Rd 1	**Honey caramel:** 5SC in magic ring[5] tighten the ring
Rd 2	INC in each st around [10]
Rd 3-5	SC in each st around [10] Change to **Off-White** in last st. Cut off **Honey caramel**
Rd 6-7	**Off-White:** SC in each st around [10]
Rd 8	SC BLO in each st around [10]
Rd 9-17	SC in each st around [10]

Cut off a thread, leaving a long tail for sewing.

STEP 2. CUFF

Rd 1	**Red:** Hold the arm upside-down and work into stitches FLO of Rd 7 SC FLO in each st around [10]
Rd 2	SC in each st around [10]

Cut off a thread and weave in

NOSE (work in continuous rounds)

Rd 1	**Honey caramel:** 6SC in magic ring [6] tighten the ring
Rd 2	INC in each st around [12]
Rd 3	*(SC in next st, INC in next st)from*rep x6 [18]
Rd 4-5	SC in each st around [18]
Rd 6	*(SC in next st, SC2tog)from*rep x6 [12]

Cut off a thread, leaving a long tail for sewing. Stuff the nose with a small amount of stuffing

BEARD (made in one piece)

1st hair	**Brown:** Chain 10; 3SC in 2nd st from hook, work across a chain: 3SC in next 7 sts, SC in next st;
2nd hair	Ch15, 3SC in 2nd st from hook, work across a chain: 3SC in next 12 sts, SC in next st;
3rd hair	Ch20, 3SC in 2nd st from hook, work across a chain: 3SC in next 17 sts, SC in next st;
4th hair	Ch15, 3SC in 2nd st from hook, work across a chain: 3SC in next 12 sts, SC in next st;
5th hair	Ch10, 3SC in 2nd st from hook, work across a chain: 3SC in next 7 sts, SC in next st.

Cut off a thread, leaving a long tail for sewing

STRAPES FOR TROUSERS
(make x2)

	Jeans Blue: Chain 12 [12]
Rd 1	SC in 2nd st from hook, SC in next 10 sts [11]

Cut off a thread leaving a long tail for sewing

SPADE

Rd 1	**Light Grey:** 6SC in magic ring [6] tighten the ring
Rd 2	INC in each st around [12]
Rd 3	SC in next 2sts, INC in each of next 2sts, SC in next 4sts, INC in each of next 2sts, SC in next 2sts [16]
Rd 4	SC in next 3sts, INC in each of next 2sts, SC in next 6sts, INC in each of next 2sts, SC in next 3sts [20]
Rd 5	SC in next 4sts, INC in each of next 2sts, SC in next 8sts, INC in each of next 2sts, SC in next 4sts [24]
Rd 6-10	SC in each st around [24]
Rd 11	SC in next 2sts, skip next 8sts, SC in next 4sts, skip next 8sts, SC in next 2sts [8]
Rd 12	SC in each st around [8] Change to **Brown** in last st. Cut off **Light Grey**, leave a long tail and leave this tail on the right side
Rd 13	**Brown:** SC BLO in each st around [8]
Rd 14-22	SC in each st around [8]

Cut off a thread, leaving a long tail for sewing

Insert a wooden stick inside of a shaft and cut the necessary length (pic.2)

HANDLE

Rd 1	**Brown:** 6SC in magic ring [6] tighten the ring
Rd 2-8	SC in each st around [6] Cut off a thread, weave in

Next, wrap a base of the shaft with gray-colored-thread to give it a nice look(pic.3)

Attach the handle to the shaft by sewing them together (pic.4-5) Result (pic.6).

BOOTS. Repeat the shoes pattern from the Lady Gardener project on page 25 with **Mustard**.

ASSEMBLING

1. Sew the beard on 8 stitches FLO of Rd 43 in front of the body under the hat brim.
2. Attach the nose, position it in the center of the face, just above the beard, and under the brim of the hat.
3. In the 44th round of the body, we have left 10 stitches (FLO) on each side specifically for attaching the arms and straps. To properly attach the arms, ensure that the stitches in the front are left available for the strap attachment. Once the arms are attached, attach the straps, and attach the bottom edge of the straps to the first Jeans Blue round of the trousers. For an added decorative touch, attach buttons at this point as well.
4. Sew the boots on the body to stitches FLO of Rd 63.
5. Make a twisted cord with **Light Green** 30cm lengh and tie on the hat. See page 18

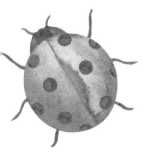

Ladybird

SIZE: 30 cm / 11.8 in

	YARN BRAND AND COLORS	TOTAL FOR A PROJECT
Red ★	Yarn Art Jeans 90	Approx. 30 g/100 meters
Black ★	Yarn Art Jeans 53	Approx. 15 g/50 meters
White ☆	Yarn Art Jeans 62	Approx. 10 g/35 meters
Honey caramel ★	Yarn Art Jeans 07	Approx. 7 g/20 meters
Bright Yellow (flower) ★	Yarn Art Jeans 35	Approx. 1g

OTHER MATERIALS	CROCHET STICHES	TOOLS
Stuffing approx. 50 g	St(s), Ch, hdc, SC, DC, INC, SC2tog, sl st, FLO, BLO, Bobble st,	Crochet hook 2.5 mm Tapestry needle

Note: Make sure to use a contrasting thread to clearly mark the beginning of each round of your project. Don't remove the thread until your work is completed.

Note: When you need to change a yarn, make sure to cut it off at the stated point. In other cases, simply drop the yarn and raise it again when needed.

STEP 1. HAT (work in continuous rounds)

Rd 1	**Red:** 6SC in magic ring [6] tighten the ring
Rd 2-13	SC in each st around [6]
Rd 14	*(SC in next st, INC in next st)from*rep x3 [9]
Rd 15	SC in each st around [9]
Rd 16	*(SC in next st, INC in next st, SC in next st)from*rep x3 [12]
Rd 17	SC in each st around [12]
Rd 18	*(SC in next 3sts, INC in next st)from*rep x3 [15]
Rd 19	SC in each st around [15]
Rd 20	*(SC in next 2sts, INC in next st, SC in next 2sts)from*rep x3[18]
Rd 21	SC in each st around [18]
Rd 22	*(SC in next 2sts, **Black:** BOBBLE in next st (work in tapestry crochet technique, it involves carrying non-working yarn inside of stitches); **Red:** SC in next 2sts, INC in next st) from*rep x3 [21] (leave Black on the wrong side)

Photo tutorial:
BOBBLE STITCH AND TAPESTRY CROCHET

complete the last stitch in previous color with the new color to start Bobble stitch: Yarn over the new color

And pull through to complete the stitch

Work 4 unfinished DC in next stitch (5 loops on your hook)

Scan for the video tutorial - Bobble Stitch

Yarn over the new color

And pull through all loops on your hook to complete the Bobble stitch

Single crochet in the next stitch carrying the non-working color inside of the stitch. Carry the yarn inside of the stitches until the next Bobble stitch.

Tapestry crochet

Rd 23	SC in each st around [21]
Rd 24	*(SC in next 3sts, INC in next st, SC in next 3sts)from*rep x3 [24]
Rd 25	SC in each st around [24]
Rd 26	*(**Black:** BOBBLE in next st, **Red:** SC in next 6sts, INC in next st) from*rep x3 [27] (leave **Black** on the wrong side)
Rd 27	SC in each st around [27]
Rd 28	*(SC in next 4sts, INC in next st, SC in next 4sts)from*rep x3 [30]
Rd 29	SC in each st around [30]
Rd 30	*(SC in next 4sts, **Black:** BOBBLE in next st, **Red:** SC in next 4sts, INC in next st) from*rep x3 [33] (leave **Black** on the wrong side)
Rd 31	SC in each st around [33]
Rd 32	*(SC in next 5sts, INC in next st, SC in next 5sts)from*rep x3 [36]
Rd 33	SC in each st around [36]
Rd 34	*(**Black:** BOBBLE in next st, **Red:** SC in next 10sts, INC in next st) from*rep x3 [39] (leave **Black** on the wrong side)
Rd 35	SC in each st around [39]

Rd 36	(SC in next 6sts, INC in next st, SC in next 6sts) from*rep x3 [42]
Rd 37	SC in each st around [42]
Rd 38	*(SC in next 6sts, **Black:** BOBBLE in next st, **Red:** SC in next 6sts, INC in next st) from*rep x3 [45]

Cut off **Black**

Rd 39	SC in each st around [45]
Rd 40	*(SC in next 7sts, INC in next st, SC in next 7sts) from*rep x3 [48]
Rd 41	SC in each st around [48]

Now that the main body of the hat is complete, it's time to start crocheting the brim (crochet the brim in joined rounds)

Rd 42	Ch2, *(DC FLO in next 7sts, 2DC FLO in next st) from*rep x2, hdc FLO in next 3sts, SC FLO in next 4sts, INC FLO in next st, SC FLO in next 4sts, hdc FLO in next 3sts, *(2DC FLO in next st, DC FLO in next 7sts)from*rep x2, 2DC FLO in next st, sl st in 2nd Ch to join the round[55]
Rd 43	Ch2, *(DC in next 4sts, 2DC in next st, DC in next 4sts) from*rep x2, hdc in next 3sts, SC in next st, INC in next st, SC in next 8sts, INC in next st, SC in next st, hdc in next 3sts, *(DC in next 4sts, 2DC in next st, DC in next 4sts)from*rep x2, sl st in 2nd Ch to join the round [61]
Rd 44	Ch2, *(DC in next 9sts, 2DC in next st)from*rep x2, DC in next 2sts, hdc in next 2sts, SC in next 5sts, INC in next st, SC in next 5sts, hdc in next 2sts, DC in next 2sts, *(2DC in next st, DC in next 9sts) from*rep x2, 2DC in next st, sl st in 2nd Ch to join the round [67]
Rd 45	Ch2, DC in next 26sts, hdc in next 2sts, SC in next 5sts, **INC** in next st, SC in next 5sts, hdc in next 2sts, DC in next 26sts, sl st in 2nd Ch to join the round [69]
Rd 46	sl st in each st around [69]. Cut off a thread and weave in

STEP 2. BODY (work in continuous rounds)

When working with a pattern, it's best to avoid cutting off the yarn while changing colors unless specifically instructed to do so.

Rd 1	**Black:** Hold the hat upside-down. Start form the first stitch of Rd 41 and work into stitches BLO: SC BLO in each st around [48]
Rd 2	SC in next 22sts, SC BLO in next 4 sts(we will attach a nose to these sts), SC in next 22sts [48]
Rd 3	SC in each st around [48] Change to **White** in last st. Do not cut off **Black**, leave it on the wrong side
Rd 4-6	**White:** SC in each st around [48] Change to **Black** in last st
Rd 7	**Black:** SC BLO in each st around [48]
Rd 8	SC in next 10sts, SC BLO in next 4 sts(stitches to attach an arm), SC in next 20sts, SC BLO in next 4sts(stitches to attach an arm), SC in next 10sts [48]
Rd 9	SC in each st around [48]Change to **White** in last st
Rd 10	**White:** SC in each st around [48]
Rd 11	*(SC in next 7sts, INC in next st) from*rep x6 [54]
Rd 12	SC in each st around [54] Change to **Black** in last st
Rd 13	**Black:** SC in each st around [54]
Rd 14	*(SC in next 4sts, INC in next st, SC in next 4sts) from*rep x6 [60]
Rd 15	SC in each st around [60] Change to **White** in last st
Rd 16	**White:** SC in each st around [60]
Rd 17	*(SC in next 7sts, INC in next st, SC in next 7sts) from*rep x4 [64]
Rd 18	SC in each st around [64] Change to **Black** in last st
	Cut off **White**
Rd 19	**Black:** SC in each st around [64]

Rd 20	*(SC BLO in next 3sts, SC2tog BLO, SC BLO in next 3sts)from*rep x8 [56]
Rd 21-22	SC in each st around [56]
	Stuff
Rd 23	*(SC in next 5sts, SC2tog)from*rep x8 [48]
Rd 24-25	SC in each st around [48]
Rd 26	SC BLO in each st around [48]

Note: we will crochet a stand on these stitches FLO later

Rd 27	SC in each st around [48]
Rd 28	*(SC in next 2sts, SC2tog, SC in next 2sts)from*rep x8 [40]
	Stuff
Rd 29	*(SC in next 3sts, SC2tog)from*rep x8 [32]
Rd 30	*(SC in next st, SC2tog, SC in next st) from*rep x8 [24]
Rd 31	*(SC in next st, SC2tog)from*rep x8 [16]
	Stuff
Rd 32	SC2tog x8 [8]

Cut off a thread. Sew the opening and weave in

STAND

| Rd 1 | Hold the body upside-down. Join **Black** yarn to the beginning of the rd 25 and work into stitches FLO: SC FLO in each st around [48]
Cut off a thread and weave in |

NOSE (work in continuous rounds)

Rd 1	**Honey caramel:** 6SC in magic ring [6] tighten the ring
Rd 2	INC in each st around [12]
Rd 3	*(SC in next st, INC in next st)from*rep x6 [18]
Rd 4-5	SC in each st around [18]
Rd 6	*(SC in next st, SC2tog)from*rep x6 [12]

Cut off a thread, leaving a long tail for sewing. Stuff the nose with a small amount of stuffing

Attach the nose by sewing or gluing it onto the body, 4 stitches FLO under the brim

Ladybird

ARMs make x2 (work in continuous rounds)

STEP 1. ARM

Rd 1	**Honey caramel:** 5SC in magic ring [5] tighten the ring
Rd 2	INC in each st around [10]
Rd 3-5	SC in each st around [10] Change to **Black** in last st. Cut off **Honey caramel**
Rd 6-7	**Black:** SC in each st around [10]
Rd 8	SC BLO in each st around [10]
Rd 9-17	SC in each st around [10]

Cut off a thread, leaving a long tail for sewing

STEP 2. CUFF

Rd 1	**Red:** Hold the arm upside-down and work into stitches FLO of Rd 7: SC FLO in each st around [10]
Rd 2	SC in each st around [10]

Cut off **Red** and weave in

LEGS (work in continuous rounds)

Rd 1	**Red:** 6SC in magic ring [6] tighten the ring
Rd 2	INC in each st around [12]
Rd 3	*(SC in next st, INC in next st)from*rep x6 [18]
Rd 4-5	SC in each st around [18]
Rd 6	*(SC in next st, SC2tog)from*rep x6 [12]

Stuff. Now to close the opening we need to squeeze it and make 6 SC inserting a hook through both layers.

Cut off a thread, leaving a long tail for sewing.
Once all other gnome parts have been assembled, attach the legs to the stand by sewing it in place.

WINGS make x2 (work in continuous rounds)

Rd 1	**Red:** 6SC in magic ring [6] tighten the ring
Rd 2	INC in each st around [12]
Rd 3	*(SC in next st, INC in next st) from*rep x6 [18]
Rd 4	*(SC in next st, INC in next st, SC in next st) from*rep x6 [24]
Rd 5	*(SC in next 3sts, INC in next st) from*rep x6 [30]
Rd 6	*(SC in next 2sts, INC in next st, SC in next 2sts) from*rep x6 [36]
Rd 7	*(SC in next 5sts, INC in next st) from*rep x6 [42]
Rd 8	*(SC in next 3sts, INC in next st, SC in next 3sts) from*rep x6 [48]
Rd 9	*(SC in next 7sts, INC in next st) from*rep x6 [54]
Row 10	Fold in half and stitch edges together by SC inserting a hook through outer legs of stiches

Cut off a thread, leave a long tail for sewing

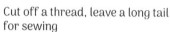

ASSEMBLING

1. Sew the arms on 4 stitches FLO of the body under the hat brim on sides.

2. Sew wings on the body right behind the arms so the top corner of the wing is attached to rd 5. Attach only the top 4 stitches of the wing.

3. Crochet Chamomile flower **White**+Yellow(disc) – see page 15. Sew or glue the flower onto the hat and watch your creation come to life!

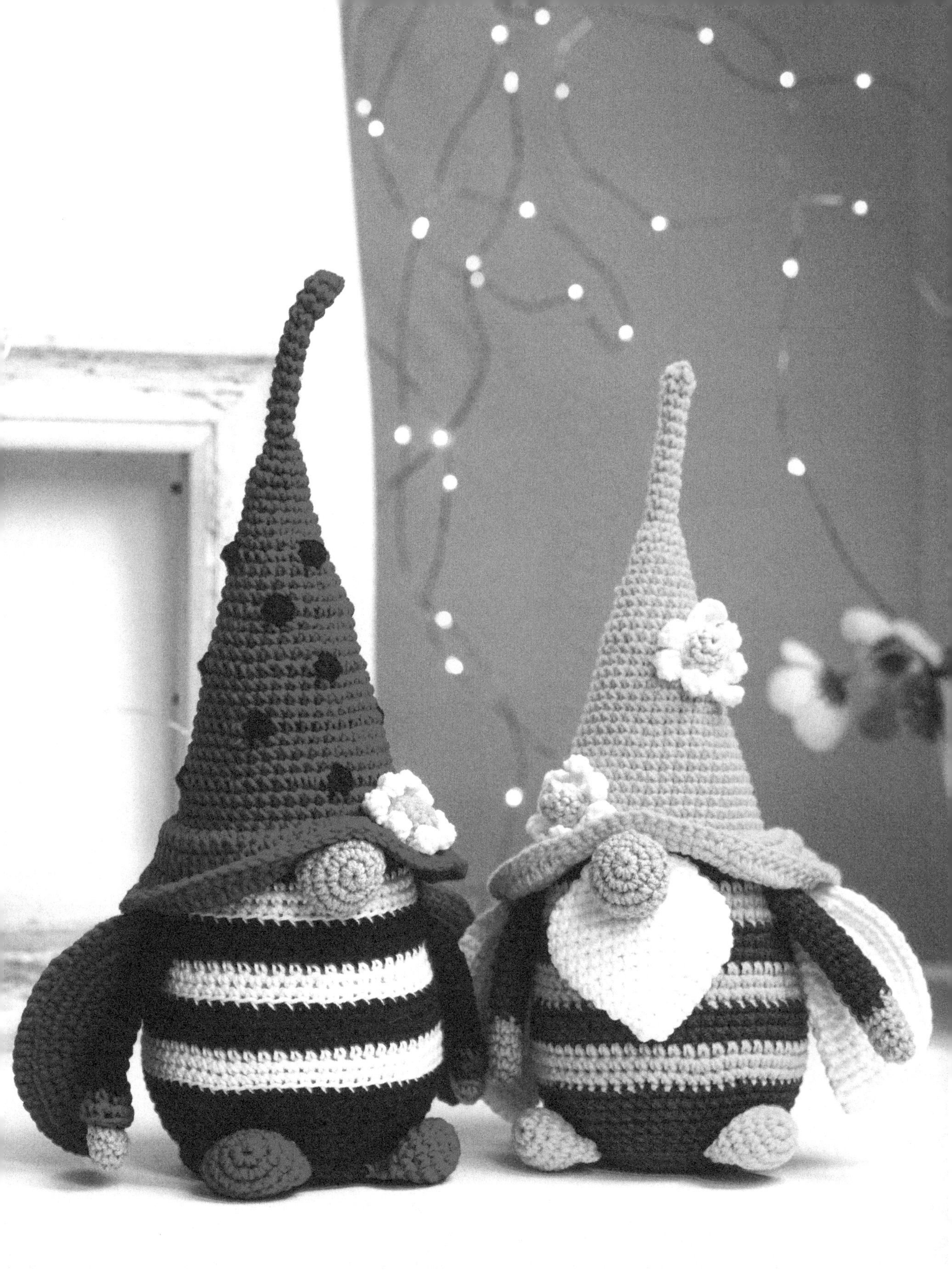

Carnation Gnome

SIZE: 25 cm / 10 in

YARN BRAND AND COLORs			TOTAL FOR A PROJECT
Red	★	Yarn Art Jeans 90	Approx. 30 g/100 meters
White	☆	Yarn Art Jeans 62	Approx. 7 g/20 meters
Honey caramel	★	Yarn Art Jeans 07	Approx. 7 g/20 meters
Light Green	★	Yarn Art Jeans 29	Approx. 10 g/35 meters
Blue	★	Yarn Art Jeans 76	Approx. 25 g/90 meters
Grass Green	★	Yarn Art Jeans 69	Approx. 10 g/35 meters

OTHER MATERIALS	CROCHET STICHES	TOOLS
Stuffing approx. 40 g	St(s), Ch, SC, INC, sl st, hdc, DC, TR, SC2tog, FLO, BLO, surface slip stitch	Crochet Hook 2.5mm Tapestry needle

Carnation

Note: To ensure that you don't miss any stitch while working on a project, it's recommended to use a contrast thread at the beginning of each round. This thread should remain in place until the item is completed.

STEP 1. HAT (work in continuous rounds)

Rd 1	**Grass Green:** 6SC in magic ring [6] tighten the ring
Rd 2-18	SC in each st around [6]
Rd 19	*(SC in next st, INC in next st)from*rep x3 [9]
Rd 20	*(SC in next st, INC in next st, SC in next st) from*rep x3 [12]
Rd 21	*(SC in next 3sts, INC in next st)from*rep x3 [15]
Rd 22	*(Ch5, sl st in 2nd st from hook, SC in next Ch, hdc in next Ch, DC in next Ch, skip next 2 sts on the main detail, sl st FLO in next st to join the leaf to the main detail)from*rep x5 (x5 leaves)
	Cut off Grass Green
Rd 23	Join **Light Green** to Rd 21 and work into stitches BLO: SC BLO in each st around [15] (pic.2)
Rd 24	*(SC in next 2sts, INC in next st, SC in next 2sts) from*rep x3 [18]
Rd 25	*(SC in next 5sts, INC in next st)from*rep x3 [21]
Rd 26	*(SC in next 3sts, INC in next st, SC in next 3sts) from*rep x3 [24]
Rd 27	SC in each st around [24] Change to Red in last st. Cut off Light Green
Rd 28	**Red:** *(SC BLO in next 7sts, INC BLO in next st)from*rep x3 [27]
Rd 29	SC in each st around [27]
Rd 30	*(SC in next 4sts, INC in next st, SC in next 4sts) from*rep x3 [30]
Rd 31	SC in each st around [30]
Rd 32	*(SC in next 9sts, INC in next st)from*rep x3 [33]
Rd 33	SC in each st around [33]
Rd 34	*(SC in next 5sts, INC in next st, SC in next 5sts) from*rep x3 [36]
Rd 35	SC in each st around [36]
Rd 36	*(SC in next 11sts, INC in next st)from*rep x3 [39]
Rd 37	SC in each st around [39]
Rd 38	*(SC in next 6sts, INC in next st, SC in next 6sts) from*rep x3 [42]
Rd 39	SC in each st around [42]
Rd 40	*(SC in next 13sts, INC in next st)from*rep x3[45]
Rd 41	SC in each st around [45]
Rd 42	(SC in next 7sts, INC in next st, SC in next 7sts) from*rep x3 [48]

Rd 43	SC in each st around [48]
Rd 44	SC BLO in each st around [48]

Note: we will crochet the second layer of petals onto these stitches FLO later

Rd 45	*(SC in next 15sts, INC in next st)from*rep x4 [52]
Rd 46	3TR FLO in each stitch around
Rd 47	*(Ch2, sl st in next)from*rep to around

Cut off Red

A second layer of "petals"

Rd 1	Hold the item upside-down, join **Red** to the beginning of Rd 43 and work into stitches FLO around: Ch3, 3TR in each stitch around, sli st in 3rd Ch
Rd 2	*(Ch2, sl st in next TR)from*rep around

Cut off Red and weave in

STEP 2. BODY (work in continuous rounds)

Rd 1	**Blue:** Hold the body upside-down. Work into stitches BLO of Rd 45: SC BLO in each st around [52]
Rd 2	SC in next 22sts, SC BLO in next 8sts(the beard with nose will be attached to these sts), SC in next 22sts [52]
Rd 3	SC in each st around [52]
Rd 4	SC in next 11sts, SC BLO in next 4sts(the arm will be attached to these sts), SC in next 22sts, SC BLO in next 4sts(the arm will be attached to these sts), SC in next 11sts [52]
Rd 5-7	SC in each st around [52]
Rd 8	(SC in next 6sts, INC in next st, SC in next 6sts) from*rep x4 [56]
Rd 9-10	SC in each st around [56]
Rd 11	*(SC in next 3sts, INC in next st, SC in next 3sts)from*rep x8 [64]
Rd 12-14	SC in each st around [64] Change to **Light Green**. Cut off **Blue**

Rd 15	**Light Green:** *(SC BLO in next 3sts, SC2tog BLO, SC BLO in next 3sts)from*rep x8 [56]
Rd 16-17	SC in each st around [56]
Rd 18	*(SC in next 5sts, SC2tog)from*rep x8 [48]

Drop the loop from your hook, we will use it later

Grass Green: work surface slip stitch into stitches of Rd 16 around (pic.4 below) Cut off **Grass Green**

Grab the **Light Green** loop back on your hook

Rd 19-20	SC in each st around [48]

Stuff

Rd 21	SC BLO in each st around [48]
Rd 22	*(SC in next 2sts, SC2tog, SC in next 2sts)from*rep x8 [40]
Rd 23	*(SC in next 3sts, SC2tog)from*rep x8 [32]
Rd 24	*(SC in next st, SC2tog, SC in next st)from*rep x8 [24]
Rd 25	*(SC in next st, SC2tog)from*rep x8 [16]

Stuff

Rd 26	SC2tog x8 [8]

Cut off a thread and sew the opening, weave in

STEP 2. STAND

Rd 1	**Grass Green:** hold the item upside-down and work into stitches FLO of Rd 20 Body (step 2), starting from the beginning of rd: SC FLO in each st around [48]

Cut off a thread and weave in

ARMs make x2 (work in continuous rounds)

| Rd 1 | **Honey caramel:** 5SC in magic ring [5] tighten the ring |

| Rd 2 | INC in each st around [10] |

| Rd 3-4 | SC in each st around [10] Change to **Blue** in last st. |

Cut off **Honey caramel**

| Rd 5-17 | **Blue:** SC in each st around [10] |

Cut off a thread, leave a long tail for sewing

BEARD (work in continuous rounds)

White: Chain 2

Rd 1	3SC in 2nd st from hook [3] (work in continuous rounds)
Rd 2	INC in each of next 3SC [6]
Rd 3	INC in each of next 2sts, SC in next 2sts, INC in next st, SC in next st [9]
Rd 4	SC in next st, INC in each of next 2sts, SC in next 5sts, INC in next st [12]
Rd 5	SC in next 2sts, INC in each of next 2sts, SC in next 5sts, INC in next st, SC in next 2sts [15]
Rd 6	SC in next 3sts, INC in each of next 2sts, SC in next 9sts, INC in next st [18]
Rd 7	SC in next 4sts, INC in each of next 2sts, SC in next 8sts, INC in next st, SC in next 3sts [21]
Rd 8	SC in next 5sts, INC in each of next 2sts, SC in next 14sts [23]
Rd 9	SC in next 6sts, INC in each of next 2sts, SC in next 14sts, INC in next st [26]
Rd 10-12	SC in each st around [26]
Rd 13	SC in next 8sts, SC2tog, SC in next 11sts, SC2tog, SC in next 3sts [24]
Rd 14	SC in next 7sts, SC2tog, SC in next 10sts, SC2tog, SC in next 3sts [22]
Rd 15	SC in next 6sts, SC2tog, SC in next 9sts, SC2tog, SC in next 3sts [20]

Cut off a thread, leaving a long tail for sewing

ANEMONE

30

NOSE (work in continuous rounds)

Rd 1	**Honey caramel:** 6SC in magic ring [6] Tighten the ring
Rd 2	INC in each st around [12]
Rd 3	*(SC in next st, INC in next st)from*rep x6 [18]
Rd 4-5	SC in each st around [18]
Rd 6	*(SC in next st, SC2tog)from*rep x6 [12]

Cut off a thread, leaving a long tail for sewing. Stuff the nose with a small amount of stuffing. Sew the nose on the beard

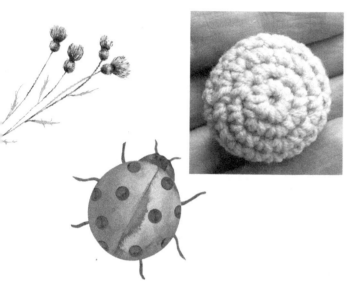

Sew the arms on the body on sides on 4 stitches FLO of Rd 3 of the body (step 2)

Sew the beard with the nose on 8 stitches FLO of Rd 1 (step 2) in front of the body uder the hat brim

Bellflower Gnome

SIZE: 25 cm / 10 in

	YARN BRAND AND COLORs	TOTAL FOR A PROJECT
Purple ★	Yarn Art Jeans 72	Approx. 15 g/50 meters
Off-White ☆	Yarn Art Jeans 03	Approx. 10 g/35 meters
Light Green ★	Yarn Art Jeans 29	Approx. 12 g/40 meters
Honey caramel ★	Yarn Art Jeans 07	Approx. 10 g/35 meters
Grass Green ★	Yarn Art Jeans 69	Approx. 12 g/40 meters
Light Blue ★	Yarn Art Jeans 75	Approx. 10g/35meters
Bright Yellow ★	Yarn Art Jeans 35	Approx. 1g(for a flower)

OTHER MATERIALS	CROCHET STICHES	TOOLS
Stuffing approx. 40 g Decorative buttons ⌀ 12 mm x2	St(s), Ch, hdc, SC, DC, INC, sl st, SC2tog, TR, BLO, FLO	Crochet Hook 2.5 mm Tapestry needle

HAT

Note: Make sure to use a contrasting thread to clearly mark the beginning of each round of your project. Don't remove the thread until your work is completed.

STEP 1. HAT

Scan for Video tutorial
- Rd 22-23

Rd 1	**Light Green:** 6SC in magic ring [6] tighten the ring
Rd 2-14	SC in each st around [6]
Rd 15	INC in each st around [12]
Rd 16	*(SC in next st, INC in next st)from*rep x6 [18]
Rd 17	*(SC in next st, INC in next st, SC in next st) from*rep x6 [24]
Rd 18	*(SC in next 3sts, INC in next st) from*rep x6 [30]

Rd 19	SC in each st around [30]
Rd 20	*(SC in next st, SC2tog)from*rep x10 [20]
Rd 21	SC in each st around [20] (pic.1)
Rd 22	*(SC FLO in next 4sts, Ch6, sl st in 2nd st from hook, sl st in next 4sts of a chain)from*rep x5 [x5 midribs], sl st in next 2 sts (replaced the beginning of round) (pic.2-3)

Rd 23	*(DC BLO in next 4 sts of 1st midribs(pic.4), 2DC in the last st of 1st midribs, TR in same st as prev st, Ch2, sl st in top of prev TR(pic.5), TR BLO in next st of 1st midribs, 2DC BLO in the same st as prev TR, DC BLO in next 4sts of 1st midribs, skip next 2sts of the edge, sl st in next st of edge (pic.6))from*rep x5 [x5 leaves, pic.7] Cut off **Light Green**, leave a long tail for sewing

STEP 2. FLOWER PART

Rd 1	Join **Purple** to the beginning of Rd 21: SC BLO in each st around [20]	Rd 12	*(SC in next 11sts, INC in next st)from*rep x4 [52]
Rd 2	*(SC in next 3sts, INC in next st)from*rep x5 [25]	Rd 13-15	SC in each st around [52]
Rd 3	*(SC in next 2sts, INC in next st, SC in next 2sts)from*rep x5 [30]	Rd 16	*(SC in next 6sts, INC in next st, SC in next 6sts)from*rep x4 [56]
Rd 4	*(SC in next 2sts, INC in next st, SC in next 2sts)from*rep **x6** [36]	Rd 17-19	SC in each st around [56]
Rd 5	*(SC in next 5sts, INC in next st)from*rep x6 [42]	Rd 20	SC FLO in each st around [56]
Rd 6	*(SC in next 3sts, INC in next st, SC in next 3sts)from*rep x6 [48]		**Note:** we will crochet stitches of a body on these stitches BLO later
Rd 7-11	SC in each st around [48]	Rd 21	*(SC in next 13sts, INC in next st) from*rep x4 [60]
		Rd 22	*(SC in next 9sts, INC in next st)from*rep x6 [66]

Rd 23: in this round we are going to make petals. See photo tutorial for a petal below
*(sl st in next st, SC in next st, hdc in next st, DC in next st, TR in next st, 2TR in next st, Chain 2, sl st in a top of TR, TR in the same st as prev TR, TR in next st, DC in next st, hdc in next st, SC in next st, sl st in next st)from*rep x6 times around to make 6 petals

Photo tutorial for a petal:

*(sl st in next st, — **1**
SC in next st, — **2**
hdc in next st, — **3**
Chain 2, — **7**
DC in next st, — **4**
TR in next st, — **5**
2TR in next st, — **6**

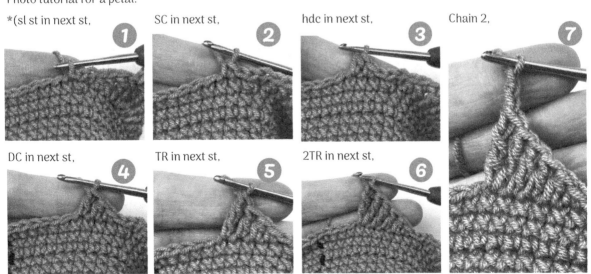

sl st in a top of TR,

8

TR in the same st as prev TR,

9

TR in next st,

10

DC in next st,

11

hdc in next st,

12

SC in next st,

13

sl st in next st)

14

Rd 24   sl st BLO in each st around. Attach the leaves to the **Purple** part with several stitches or just glue it.

BODY (work in continuous rounds)

Rd 1	**Off-White:** Hold the hat upside-down and work into stitches BLO of Rd 19 of step 2 starting from the beginning of rd: SC BLO in each st around [56]
Rd 2	SC in next 12sts, SC BLO in next 6sts(the arm and straps for trousers will be attach to these sts), SC in next 6sts, SC BLO in next 8sts(the nose and beard will be attach to these sts), SC in next 6sts, SC BLO in next 6sts(the arm and straps for trousers will be attach to these sts), SC in next 12sts [56]
Rd 3-7	SC in each st around [56]
Rd 8	*(SC in next 13sts, INC in next st)from*rep x4 [60]

Rd 9-10   SC in each st around [60]

Rd 11   *(SC in next 7sts, INC in next st, SC in next 7sts) from*rep x4 [64] Change to **Light Green** in last st. Cut off **Off-White**

Rd 12   **Light Green:** SC BLO in each st around [64]

Rd 13-14   SC in each st around [64] Change to **Grass green** in last st. Cut off Light Green

Rd 15   **Grass Green:** *(SC BLO in next 3sts, SC2tog BLO, SC BLO in next 3sts)from*rep x8 [56]

Rd 16-18   SC in each st around [56]

Rd 19   *(SC in next 5sts, SC2tog)from*rep x8 [48]

Stuff

Rd 20-21   SC in each st around [48]

Rd 22   SC BLO in each st around [48]

Note: we will crochet a stand on these stitches FLO later

Rd 23   *(SC in next 2sts, SC2tog, SC in next 2sts)from*rep x8 [40]

Rd 24   *(SC in next 3sts, SC2tog)from*rep x8 [32]

Rd 25   *(SC in next st, SC2tog, SC in next st)from*rep x8 [24]

Rd 26   *(SC in next st, SC2tog)from*rep x8 [16]

Stuff

Rd 27   SC2tog x8 [8]

Cut off a thread and sew the opening

ARMs make x2
(work in continuous rounds)

Rd 1   **Honey caramel:** 5SC in magic ring [5] Tighten the ring

Rd 2   INC in each st around [10]

Rd 3-5   SC in each st around [10] Change to **Off-White** in last st.

Cut off **Honey caramel**

Rd 6-17   **Off-White:** SC in each st around [10]

Cut off a thread, leaving a long tail for sewing

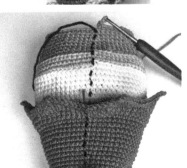

BEARD (work in continuous rounds)

Rd 1   **Light Blue:** 4SC in magic ring [4] tighten the ring

Rd 2   *(SC in next st, INC in next st)from*rep x2 [6]

Rd 3   INC in each of next 2sts, SC in next 2sts, INC in next st, SC in next st [9]

Rd 4   SC in next st, INC in each of next 2sts, SC in next 5sts, INC in next st [12]

Rd 5   SC in next 2sts, INC in each of next 2sts, SC in next 5sts, INC in next st, SC in next 2sts [15]

Rd 6   SC in next 3sts, INC in each of next 2sts, SC in next 9sts, INC in next st [18]

Rd 7   SC in next 4sts, INC in each of next 2sts, SC in next 8sts, INC in next st, SC in next 3sts [21]

Rd 8   SC in next 5sts, INC in each of next 2sts, SC in next 14sts [23]

Rd 9   SC in next 6sts, INC in each of next 2sts, SC in next 14sts, INC in next st [26]

Rd 10-12   SC in each st around [26]

Rd 13   SC in next 8sts, SC2tog, SC in next 11sts, SC2tog, SC in next 3sts [24]

Rd 14   SC in next 7sts, SC2tog, SC in next 10sts, SC2tog, SC in next 3sts [22]

Rd 15-17   SC in each st around [22]

Cut off a thread, leaving a long tail for sewing

NOSE (work in continuous rounds)

Rd 1	**Honey caramel:** 6SC in magic ring [6] Tighten the ring
Rd 2	INC in each st around [12]
Rd 3	*(SC in next st, INC in next st)from*rep x6 [18]
Rd 4-5	SC in each st around [18]
Rd 6	*(SC in next st, SC2tog)from*rep x6 [12]

Cut off a thread, leaving a long tail for sewing. Stuff the nose with a small amount of stuffing. Sew the nose on the beard

BOOTS make x2 (work in continuous rounds)

	Light Green: Chain 2
Rd 1	3SC in 2ⁿᵈ st from hook [3] work in the round
Rd 2	INC in each of next 3SC [6]
Rd 3	INC in each of next 2sts, SC in next 2sts, INC in next st, SC in next st [9]
Rd 4	SC in next st, INC in each of next 2sts, SC in next 4sts, INC in next st, SC in next st [12]
Rd 5	SC in next 2sts, INC in each of next 2sts, SC in next 8sts [14]
Rd 6	SC in next 3sts, INC in each of next 2sts, SC in next 9sts [16]
Rd 7	SC in next 4sts, INC in each of next 2sts, SC in next 10sts [18]
Rd 8-9	SC in each st around [18]
Rd 10	SC in next st, SC2tog x6, SC in next 5 sts [12]
Rd 11	sl st in next 2sts, Stuff the boot

Now to close the opening we need to squeeze it and make SCs inserting a hook through both sides (total is 6SC). Cut off a thread, leaving a long tail for sewing.

STRAPS FOR TROUSERS make x2

	Grass Green: Chain 12
Row 1	SC in 2ⁿᵈ st from hook, SC in next 10 sts [11]

Cut off a thread, leaving a long tail for sewing

1. Sew the beard with the nose to 8 stitches FLO of Rd 2 of the body in front under the hat brim.

2. There are 6 available stitches (FLO) on each side we have made for the arm and straps to attach in Rd 2 of the body. You need to attach each arm the way the stitches in front will be left available for attaching the straps. Attach the bottom end of the straps to the **Light Green** round of the body and attach the decorative buttons.

3. Sew the boots on the body Rd 21 stitches FLO

Crochet Chamomile flower **Light Blue**+Yellow(disc) – see page 15. Attach (sew or glue) on the gnome's hat

Blue Hat Sunflower Gnome

SIZE: 26 cm / 10 in

YARN BRAND AND COLORs			TOTAL FOR A PROJECT
Blue	☆	Yarn Art Jeans 76	Approx. 20 g/70 meters
Brown	★	Yarn Art Jeans 40	Approx. 15 g/50 meters
Wheat	☆	Yarn Art Jeans 05	Approx. 5 g/15 meters
Off-White	☆	Yarn Art Jeans 03	Approx. 7 g/20 meters
Bright Yellow	★	Yarn Art Jeans 35	Approx. 3 g/10 meters
Grass Green	★	Yarn Art Jeans 69	Approx. 3 g/10 meters

OTHER MATERIALS	CROCHET STICHES	TOOLS
Stuffing approx. 50 g	St(s), Ch, SC, hdc, DC, TR, INC, sl st, SC2tog, BLO, FLO, surface slip stitch	Crochet Hook 2.5 mm Tapestry needle

Note: Make sure to use a contrasting thread to clearly mark the beginning of each round of your project. Don't remove the thread until your work is completed.

HAT (work in continuous rounds)

Rd 1	**Blue:** 6SC in magic ring [6] tighten the ring
Rd 2	*(INC in next st, SC in next st)from*rep x3 [9]
Rd 3-12	SC in each st around [9]
Rd 13	*(SC in next st, INC in next st, SC in next st) from*rep x3 [12]
Rd 14	SC in each st around [12]
Rd 15	*(SC in next 3sts, INC in next st)from*rep x3 [15]
Rd 16	SC in each st around [15]
Rd 17	*(SC in next 2sts, INC in next st, SC in next 2sts) from*rep x3 [18]
Rd 18	SC in each st around [18]
Rd 19	*(SC in next 5sts, INC in next st)from*rep x3 [21]
Rd 20	SC in each st around [21]
Rd 21	*(SC in next 3sts, INC in next st, SC in next 3sts) from*rep x3 [24]
Rd 22	SC in each st around [24]
Rd 23	*(SC in next 7sts, INC in next st)from*rep x3 [27]
Rd 24	SC in each st around [27]
Rd 25	*(SC in next 4sts, INC in next st, SC in next 4sts) from*rep x3 [30]
Rd 26	SC in each st around [30]
Rd 27	*(SC in next 9sts, INC in next st)from*rep x3 [33]
Rd 28	SC in each st around [33]
Rd 29	*(SC in next 5sts, INC in next st, SC in next 5sts) from*rep x3 [36]
Rd 30	SC in each st around [36]
Rd 31	*(SC in next 11sts, INC in next st)from*rep x3 [39]
Rd 32	SC in each st around [39]
Rd 33	*(SC in next 6sts, INC in next st, SC in next 6sts) from*rep x3 [42]
Rd 34	SC in each st around [42]
Rd 35	*(SC in next 13sts, INC in next st)from*rep x3 [45]

Rd 36	SC in each st around [45]
Rd 37	*(SC in next 7sts, INC in next st, SC in next 7sts) from*rep x3 [48]
Rd 38	SC in each st around [48]
Rd 39	*(SC in next 15sts, INC in next st)from*rep x3 [51]
Rd 40	SC in each st around [51]
Rd 41	*(SC in next 8sts, INC in next st, SC in next 8sts) from*rep x3 [54]
Rd 42	*(SC in next 26sts, INC in next st)from*rep x2 [56]
Rd 43-45	SC in each st around [56]

Continue - HAT BRIM (work in joined rounds)

Rd 46	Ch2, *(DC FLO in next 6sts, 2DC FLO in next st) from*rep x3, hdc FLO in next st, SC FLO in next 5sts, INC FLO in next st, SC FLO in next 5sts, hdc FLO in next st, *(2DC FLO in next st, DC FLO in next 6sts)from*rep x3, DC FLO in next st, sl st in 2nd Ch [64]
Rd 47	Ch2, DC in next 25sts, hdc in next st, SC in next 12sts, hdc in next st, DC in next 24sts, sl st in 2nd Ch [64]
Rd 48	Ch2, *(DC in next 7sts, 2DC in next st)from*rep x3, hdc in next st, SC in next 6sts, INC in next st, SC in next 6sts, hdc in next st, *(2DC in next st, DC in next 7sts) from*rep x3, DC in next st, sl st in 2nd Ch [72]
Rd 49	SC in next 72sts around[72], sl st in 1st stitch of rd

Cut off **Blue** and weave in

BODY (work in continuous rounds)

Rd 1	Hold the hat upside-down, with **Brown** work into stitches BLO of Rd 45, start from the beginning of rd: SC BLO in each st around [56]
Rd 2	SC in next 11sts, SC BLO in next 5sts (the arm will be attached to these sts), SC in next 8sts, SC BLO in next 8sts (the beard will be attached to these sts), SC in next 8sts, SC BLO in next 5sts (the arm will be attached to these sts), SC in next 11sts [56]
Rd 3-7	SC in each st around [56]
Rd 8	*(SC in next 13sts, INC in next st)from*rep x4 [60]
Rd 9-12	SC in each st around [60]
Rd 13	*(SC in next 7sts, INC in next st, SC in next 7sts) from*rep x4 [64]

Rd 14-15	SC in each st around [64]. Change to **Blue** in last stitch. Cut off **Brown**
Rd 16	**Blue:** *(SC BLO in next 3sts, SC2tog BLO, SC BLO in next 3sts)from*rep x8 [56]
Rd 17-18	SC in each st around [56]
	Drop a loop from your hook we will use it later
	Bright Yellow: work surface slip stitch into stitches of Rd 16
	Cut off **Bright Yellow** and weave in
Rd 19	Grab a dropped **Blue** loop back on your hook and continue: *(SC in next 5sts, SC2tog)from*rep x8 [48]
	Stuff
Rd 20-21	SC in each st around [48]
Rd 22	SC BLO in each st around [48]
	Note: we will crochet the stand into these sts FLO later
Rd 23	*(SC in next 2sts, SC2tog, SC in next 2sts)from*rep x8 [40]
Rd 24	*(SC in next 3sts, SC2tog)from*rep x8 [32]
Rd 25	*(SC in next st, SC2tog, SC in next st)from*rep x8 [24]
Rd 26	*(SC in next st, SC2tog)from*rep x8 [16]
	Stuff
Rd 27	SC2tog x8 [8]
	Cut off a thread and sew the opening, weave in

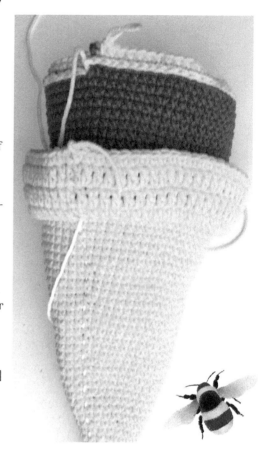

STAND

Rd 1	Hold the body upside-down, with **Bright Yellow** work into stitches FLO of Rd 21 of the Body: SC FLO in each st around [48]. Cut off a thread and weave in

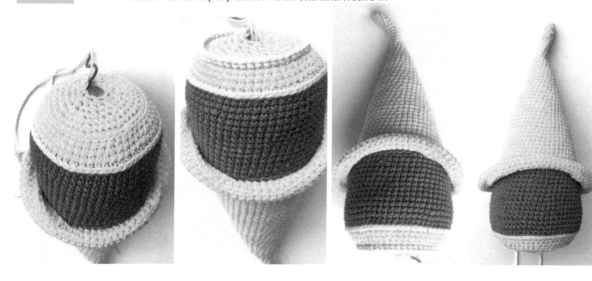

BEARD (work in continuous rounds)

Off-White: Chain 2 [2]

Rd 1	3SC in 2nd st from hook [3] (work in continuous rounds)
Rd 2	INC in each of 3SC [6]
Rd 3	INC in each of next 2sts, SC in next 2sts, INC in next st, SC in next st [9]
Rd 4	SC in next st, INC in each of next 2sts, SC in next 5sts, INC in next st [12]
Rd 5	SC in next 2sts, INC in each of next 2sts, SC in next 5sts, INC in next st, SC in next 2sts [15]
Rd 6	SC in next 3sts, INC in each of next 2sts, SC in next 9sts, INC in next st [18]
Rd 7	SC in next 4sts, INC in each of next 2sts, SC in next 8sts, INC in next st, SC in next 3sts [21]
Rd 8	SC in next 5sts, INC in each of next 2sts, SC in next 14sts [23]
Rd 9	SC in next 6sts, INC in each of next 2sts, SC in next 14sts, INC in next st [26]
Rd 10-12	SC in each st around [26]
Rd 13	SC in next 8sts, SC2tog, SC in next 11sts, SC2tog, SC in next 3sts [24]
Rd 14	SC in next 7sts, SC2tog, SC in next 10sts, SC2tog, SC in next 3sts [22]
Rd 15	SC in next 6sts, SC2tog, SC in next 9sts, SC2tog, SC in next 3sts [20]
Rd 16	SC in each st around [20]

Cut off a thread, leaving a long tail for sewing

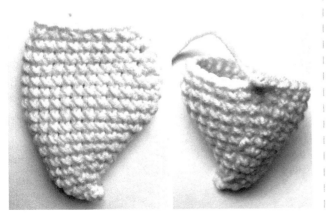

ARMs (make x2, work in continuous rounds)

Rd 1	**Wheat:** 5SC in magic ring [5] tighten the ring
Rd 2	INC in each st around [10]
Rd 3-5	SC in each st around [10]

Change to **Brown** in last st. Cut off Wheat

Rd 6-7	**Brown:** SC in each st around [10]
Rd 8	SC BLO in each st around [10]
Rd 9-17	SC in each st around [10]

Cut off a thread, leaving a long tail for sewing.

NOSE (work in continuous rounds)

Rd 1	**Wheat:** 6SC in magic ring [6] tighten the ring
Rd 2	INC in each st around [12]
Rd 3	*(SC in next st, INC in next st)from*rep x6 [18]
Rd 4-5	SC in each st around [18]
Rd 6	*(SC in next st, SC2tog)from*rep x6 [12]

Cut off a thread, leaving a long tail for sewing. Stuff the nose with a small amount of stuffing

SUNFLOWER

Rd 1	**Brown:** in magic ring: Ch2, 11DC, sl st in Ch 2nd st of rd. Cut off a thread

Petal:

Join **Bright Yellow:**	1) Chain 3 (count as 1 DC)	2) 4DC in next st	3) Drop a loop from your hook

Rd 2

4) Inset a hook into 3rd Chain. (**Note:**When you will wok other petals insert your hook in 1st DC)	5) And insert the hook back into the dropped loop	6) Yarn over and pull through both loops on your hook. Petal is done.	Now work to end (Ch2, repeat Petal) around, and sl st at the end (total is 12 petals). Cut off a thread

Rd 3	Join **Grass Green** and make leaves: Ch1, *(all in next 2Ch-space: [hdc, 2DC, TR, Ch4, sl st in previous TR, continue in 2ch-space: TR, 2DC, hdc], SC in next 2Ch-space)from*rep x6.Total is 6 leaves

ASSEMBLING

Attach (sew /glue) the nose on the beard and then sew on 8 stitches FLO made in front of the body under the hat brim.

Sew the arms on the body under the hat brim on 5 stitches you've left on Rd 1 of the body.

To add a creative touch to your hat make a twisted cord that measures approximately 30cm in length and tie it onto the hat.

Attach the flower to the hat using either sewing or glue.

Poppy Gnome

SIZE: 25 cm / 10 in

	YARN BRAND AND COLORs		TOTAL FOR A PROJECT
Red	★	Yarn Art Jeans 90	Approx. 25 g/90 meters
Black	★	Yarn Art Jeans 53	Approx. 30 g/100 meters
White	☆	Yarn Art Jeans 62	Approx. 7 g/20 meters
Honey caramel	★	Yarn Art Jeans 07	Approx. 7 g/20 meters
Light Green	★	Yarn Art Jeans 29	Approx. 15 g/55 meters

OTHER MATERIALS	CROCHET STICHES	TOOLS
Stuffing approx. 50 g	St(s), Ch, SC, hdc, INC, DC, TR, sl st, SC2tog, FLO, BLO, DC2tog	Crochet hook 2.5 mm Tapestry needle

Note: Make sure to use a contrasting thread to clearly mark the beginning of each round of your project. Don't remove the thread until your work is completed.

STEP 1. HAT + BODY (work in continuous rounds)

Rd 1	**Light Green:** 6SC in magic ring [6] tighten the ring
Rd 2-17	SC in each st around [6]
Rd 18	*(SC in next st, INC in next st)from*rep x3 [9]
Rd 19	*(SC in next st, INC in next st, SC in next st)from*rep x3 [12]
Rd 20	*(SC in next 3sts, INC in next st)from*rep x3 [15]
Rd 21	*(SC in next 2sts, INC in next st, SC in next 2sts) from*rep x3 [18]
Rd 22	*(SC in next 5sts, INC in next st)from*rep x3 [21]
Rd 23	*(SC in next 3sts, INC in next st, SC in next 3sts) from*rep x3 [24]
Rd 24	*(SC BLO in next 7sts, INC BLO in next st)from*rep x3 [27] Change to **Black** in last st. Cut off **Light Green**
Rd 25	**Black:** SC BLO in each st around [27]

Note: Petals will be attached to these stitches FLO later

Rd 26	*(SC in next 4sts, INC in next st, SC in next 4sts) from*rep x3[30]
Rd 27	SC in each st around [30]
Rd 28	*(SC in next 9sts, INC in next st)from*rep x3 [33]
Rd 29	SC in each st around [33]
Rd 30	*(SC in next 5sts, INC in next st, SC in next 5sts) from*rep x3 [36]
Rd 31	SC in each st around [36]
Rd 32	*(SC in next 11sts, INC in next st)from*rep x3 [39]
Rd 33	SC in each st around [39]
Rd 34	*(SC in next 6sts, INC in next st, SC in next 6sts) from*repx3[42]
Rd 35	SC in each st around [42]
Rd 36	*(SC in next 13sts, INC in next st)from*rep x3 [45]
Rd 37	SC BLO in each st around [45]

Note: in step 3, we will crochet a brim of the hat to these stitches FLO

Rd 38	(SC in next 7sts, INC in next st, SC in next 7sts) from*rep x3 [48]
Rd 39	SC in next 20 sts, SC BLO in next 8 sts(the bear with nose will be attached to these sts), SC in next 20 sts [48]
Rd 40	SC in each st around [48]
Rd 41	SC in next 10sts, SC BLO in next 4 sts(the arm will be attached to these sts), SC in next 20sts, SC BLO in next 4sts(the arm will be attached to these sts), SC in next 10sts [48]
Rd 42-48	SC in each st around [48]
Rd 49	*(SC in next 7sts, INC in next st)from*rep x6 [54]
Rd 50-51	SC in each st around [54]
Rd 52	*(SC in next 4sts, INC in next st, SC in next 4sts) from*rep x6 [60]
Rd 53-54	SC in each st around [60]
Rd 55	*(SC in next 7sts, INC in next st, SC in next 7sts) from*rep x4 [64]
Rd 56-57	SC in each st around [64]
Rd 58	*(SC in next 3sts, SC2tog, SC in next 3sts)from*rep x8 [56]
Rd 59	SC in each st around [56] Change to **Light Green** in last st. Cut off **Black**
Rd 60	**Light Green:** work regular and long SC in chaotic manner to imitate grass. SC in each st around [56]
Rd 61	*(SC in next 5sts, SC2tog)from*rep x8 [48]
Rd 62-63	SC in each st around [48]
Rd 64	SC BLO in each st around [48]

Note: in step 2, we will work a stand on these stitches FLO

Rd 65	SC in each st around [48]
Rd 66	*(SC in next 2sts, SC2tog, SC in next 2sts)from*rep x8 [40]
	Stuff
Rd 67	*(SC in next 3sts, SC2tog)from*rep x8 [32]
Rd 68	*(SC in next st, SC2tog, SC in next st)from*rep x8 [24]
Rd 69	*(SC in next st, SC2tog)from*rep x8 [16]
	Stuff
Rd 70	SC2tog x8 [8]
	Cut off a thread. Sew the opening and weave in

STEP 2. STAND

Rd 1	**Light Green** hold the item upside-down and work into stitches FLO of Rd 63 Body, starting from the beginning of rd: SC FLO in each st around [48] (pic.1) Cut off a thread and weave in

STEP 3. HAT BRIM

Rd 1	**Black:** hold the body upside-down, starting from the beginning of rd work into stitches FLO of Rd 36: Ch2, 2DC in each stitch around, sl st in Ch2 of rd. Cut off a thread and weave in (pic. 2-3)
Rd 2	Join **White:** *(Ch2, sl st in next st)from*rep around. Cut off a thread and weave in(pic.4)

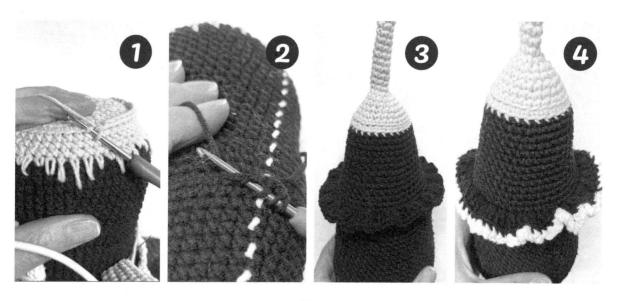

PETALS (make 3)
(worked in rows; do not count turning chain)

	Red: Chain 14 [14]
Row 1	2DC in 3rd st from hook, DC in next 6sts, hdc in next 3sts, SC in next 2sts [13] Ch1(turning chain), Turn
Row 2	SC in next 3sts, hdc in next 3sts, DC in next 7sts [13], Ch2(turning chain), Turn
Row 3	2DC in same st as Ch2, DC in next 6sts, hdc in next 3sts, SC in next 3sts [14], Ch1, Turn
Row 4	SC in next 3sts, hdc in next 3sts, DC in next 8sts [14] Ch2, Turn
Row 5	DC in same st as Ch2, DC in next 7sts, hdc in next 3sts, SC in next 3sts [14], Ch1, Turn
Row 6	SC in next 3sts, hdc in next 3sts, DC in next 8sts [14], Ch2, Turn
Row 7	2DC in same st as Ch2, DC in next 7sts, hdc in next 3sts, SC in next 3sts [15] Ch1, Turn
Row 8	SC in next 4sts, hdc in next 3sts, DC in next 8sts [15] Ch2, Turn
Row 9	DC in same st as Ch2, DC in next 7sts, hdc in next 3sts, SC in next 4 sts [15] Ch1, Turn
Row 10	SC in next 4 sts, hdc in next 3sts, DC in next 8sts [15], Ch2, Turn
Row 11	DC in same st as Ch2, DC in next 7 sts, hdc in next 3sts, SC in next 4sts [15], Ch1, Turn
Row 12	SC in next 3sts, hdc in next 3sts, DC in next 7sts, DC2tog [14], Ch2 Turn
Row 13	DC in same st as Ch2, DC in next 7sts, hdc in next 3sts, SC in next 3sts [14], Ch1, Turn
Row 14	SC in next 3sts, hdc in next 3sts, DC in next 8sts [14], Ch2, Turn
Row 15	DC in same st as Ch2, DC in next 7sts, hdc in next 3sts, SC in next 3sts [14], Ch1, Turn
Row 16	SC in next 3sts, hdc in next 2sts, DC in next 7sts, DC2tog [13], Ch2, Turn
Row 17	DC in same st as Ch2, DC in next 7 sts, hdc in next 2 sts, SC in next 3 sts [13], Ch1, Turn
Row 18	SC in next 2 sts, hdc in next 2sts, DC in next 7sts, DC2tog [12]

Cut off a thread. Make 3 petals. For the 3rd petal do not Cut off a thread.

1.1

Continue crocheting into the side short edge of petal #3:
1) SC in next 2rows, then work SC in each second row to gather the edge (total is 7 SC); 2 rows are left for joining the second petal;
2) Join the second petal: inserting your hook through both layers of 2 petals, work SC in the next 2 rows.
3) continue on the edge of the second petal work in the same way as for the first petal: SC in each second row to gather the edge (total is 7 SC); 2 rows are left for joining the third petal; pic.1.1 on the prev page.
4) Join the third petal: inserting your hook through both layers of 2 petals work SC in the next 2 rows.
5) continue on the edge of the third petal work in the same way as for the first 2 petals: SC in each second row to gather the edge (total is 7 SC); 2 rows are left for joining the third and first petals;
6) join the third and first petals together, inserting your hook through both layers: work SC in the 2 rows/stitches. Result pic.1

Put this detail on the hat and sew on stitches FLO of Rd 24 by a tapestry needle(pic.2).

Now we need to cover the seam with **Light Green:** Starting from the beginning of the round, we will now work in stitches FLO of Round 23 (this is the round above the one where we attached the petals): *(hdc FLO in next 5 sts, 2hdc FLO in next st) from*rep x4 [24] (pic.3)

Attach the **Light Green** round to the petals, employing a running stitch. This will prevent the round from protruding and create a cohesive finish. (pic.4)

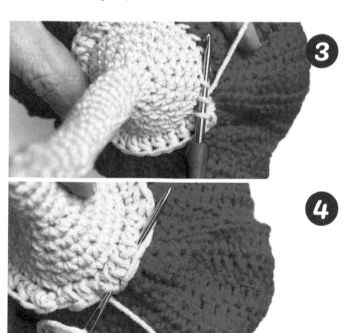

ARMs (make x2, work in continuous rounds)

STEP 1. ARM

Rd 1	**Honey caramel:** 5SC in magic ring [5] tighten the ring
Rd 2	INC in each st around [10]
Rd 3-5	SC in each st around [10] Change to **Light Green** in last st. Cut off **Honey caramel**
Rd 6-7	**Light Green:** SC in each st around [10]
Rd 8	SC BLO in each st around [10]
Rd 9-17	SC in each st around [10]

Cut off a thread, leaving a long tail for sewing

STEP 2. CUFF

Rd 1	**Red:** Hold the arm upside-down and work into stitches FLO of Rd 7: SC FLO in each st around [10]
Rd 2	SC in each st around [10]

Cut off a thread and weave in

NOSE (work in continuous rounds)

Rd 1	**Honey caramel:** 6SC in magic ring [6] tighten the ring
Rd 2	INC in each st around [12]
Rd 3	*(SC in next st, INC in next st)from*rep x6 [18]
Rd 4-5	SC in each st around [18]
Rd 6	*(SC in next st, SC2tog)from*rep x6 [12]

Cut off a thread, leaving a long tail for sewing. Stuff the nose with a small amount of stuffing

BOOTS (work in continuous rounds)

Rd 1	**Light Green:** 6SC in magic ring [6] tighten the ring
Rd 2	INC in each st around [12]
Rd 3	*(SC in next st, INC in next st)from*rep x6 [18]
Rd 4-5	SC in each st around [18]
Rd 6	*(SC in next st, SC2tog)from*rep x6 [12]

Stuff. Now to close the opening we need to squeeze it and make 6 SC inserting a hook through both sides.

Cut off a thread, leaving a long tail for sewing.

BEARD (work in continuous rounds)

White: Chain 2 [2]

Rd 1	3SC in 2nd st from hook [3] (work in continuous rounds)
Rd 2	INC in each of next 3SC [6]
Rd 3	INC in each of next 2sts, SC in next 2sts, INC in next st, SC in next st [9]
Rd 4	SC in next st, INC in each of next 2sts, SC in next 5sts, INC in next st [12]
Rd 5	SC in next 2sts, INC in each of next 2sts, SC in next 5sts, INC in next st, SC in next 2sts [15]
Rd 6	SC in next 3sts, INC in each of next 2sts, SC in next 9sts, INC in next st [18]
Rd 7	SC in next 4sts, INC in each of next 2sts, SC in next 8sts, INC in next st, SC in next 3sts [21]
Rd 8	SC in next 5sts, INC in each of next 2sts, SC in next 14sts [23]
Rd 9	SC in next 6sts, INC in each of next 2sts, SC in next 14sts, INC in next st [26]
Rd 10-12	SC in each st around [26]
Rd 13	SC in next 8sts, SC2tog, SC in next 11sts, SC2tog, SC in next 3sts [24]
Rd 14	SC in next 7sts, SC2tog, SC in next 10sts, SC2tog, SC in next 3sts [22]
Rd 15	SC in next 6sts, SC2tog, SC in next 9sts, SC2tog, SC in next 3sts [20]

Cut off a thread, leave a long tail for sewing. Sew the nose on the beard(pic. 2-3)

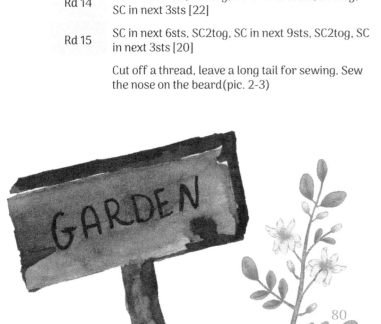

Poppy Gnome

Rd 1: **Light Green:** 5SC in magic ring [5] tighten the ring a bit, leave an opening about 4mm

Slip stitch in 1st SC of rd

Rd 2: Ch1, 10DC in magic ring, sl st in 1st st of rd. Cut off a thread and weave in.

Rd 3: **Black:** *(Ch1, sl st FLO in next st)from*rep to end. Cut off a thread and weave in.

Rd 4: **Red:** Join to the 1st stitch BLO of Rd 2 and work: *(Ch4, skip next st, SC in BLO in next st) from*rep around

Rd 5: *(Ch3, 5TR in 4Ch-space, Ch3, sl st in next SC)from*rep around

Cut off a thread, leaving a long tail for sewing

ASSEMBLING

1. Sew the nose with beard on 8 stitches FLO of Rd 38 in front of the body under the hat brim.
2. Sew arms on 4 stitches FLO of Rd 40 under the hat brim on both sides.
3. Sew the boots on the stand.
4. Sew the poppy flower on the body.

Bumblebee Gnome

SIZE: 30 cm / 12 in

YARN BRAND AND COLORs			TOTAL FOR A PROJECT
Dark Brown	★	Yarn Art Jeans 70	Approx. 15 g/50 meters
Bright Yellow	★	Yarn Art Jeans 35	Approx. 25 g/90 meters
Honey caramel	★	Yarn Art Jeans 07	Approx. 7 g/20 meters
White	☆	Yarn Art Jeans 62	Approx. 15 g/50 meters
Light Blue	★	Yarn Art Jeans 75	2 g for flowers

OTHER MATERIALS	CROCHET STICHES	TOOLS
Stuffing approx. 50 g	St(s), Ch, SC, hdc, INC, DC, sl st, SC2tog, FLO, BLO	Crochet hook 2.5 mm Tapestry needle Stitch marker

Bumblebee

Note: Make sure to use a contrasting thread to clearly mark the beginning of each round of your project. Don't remove the thread until your work is completed.

Note: When you need to change a yarn, make sure to cut it off at the stated point. In other cases, simply drop the yarn and raise it again when needed.

STEP 1. HAT (work in continuous rounds)

Rd 1	**Bright Yellow:** 6SC in magic ring [6] tighten the ring
Rd 2-13	SC in each st around [6]
Rd 14	*(SC in next st, INC in next st)from*rep x3 [9]
Rd 15	SC in each st around [9]
Rd 16	*(SC in next st, INC in next st, SC in next st) from*rep x3 [12]
Rd 17	SC in each st around [12]
Rd 18	*(SC in next 3sts, INC in next st)from*rep x3 [15]
Rd 19	SC in each st around [15]
Rd 20	*(SC in next 2sts, INC in next st, SC in next 2sts) from*rep x3 [18]
Rd 21	SC in each st around [18]
Rd 22	*(SC in next 5sts, INC in next st)from*rep x3 [21]
Rd 23	SC in each st around [21]
Rd 24	*(SC in next 3sts, INC in next st, SC in next 3sts) from*rep x3 [24]
Rd 25	SC in each st around [24]
Rd 26	*(SC in next 7sts, INC in next st)from*rep x3 [27]
Rd 27	SC in each st around [27]
Rd 28	*(SC in next 4sts, INC in next st, SC in next 4sts) from*rep x3 [30]
Rd 29	SC in each st around [30]
Rd 30	*(SC in next 9sts, INC in next st)from*rep x3 [33]
Rd 31	SC in each st around [33]
Rd 32	*(SC in next 5sts, INC in next st, SC in next 5sts) from*rep x3 [36]
Rd 33	SC in each st around [36]
Rd 34	*(SC in next 11sts, INC in next st)from*rep x3 [39]
Rd 35	SC in each st around [39]
Rd 36	(SC in next 6sts, INC in next st, SC in next 6sts) from*rep x3 [42]
Rd 37	SC in each st around [42]

Rd 38	*(SC in next 13sts, INC in next st)from*rep x3 [45]
Rd 39	SC in each st around [45]
Rd 40	*(SC in next 7sts, INC in next st, SC in next 7sts)from*rep x3 [48]
Rd 41	SC in each st around [48] Mark this round by placing a stitch marker into last stitch. In step 2, we will be crocheting the body to these stitches BLO

The hat is completed, start working on the hat brim (crocheted in joined rounds)

Rd 42	Ch2, *(DC FLO in next 7sts, 2DC FLO in next st) from*rep x2, hdc FLO in next 3sts, SC FLO in next 4sts, INC FLO in next st, SC FLO in next 4sts, hdc FLO in next 3sts, *(2DC FLO in next st, DC FLO in next 7sts)from*rep x2, 2DC FLO in next st, sl st in 2nd Ch to join the round [55]
Rd 43	Ch2, *(DC in next 4sts, 2DC in next st, DC in next 4sts) from*rep x2, hdc in next 3sts, SC in next st, INC in next st, SC in next 8 sts, INC in next st, SC in next st, hdc in next 3sts, *(DC in next 4sts, 2DC in next st, DC in next 4sts) from*rep x2, sl st in 2nd Ch to join the round [61]
Rd 44	Ch2, *(DC in next 9sts, 2DC in next st) from*rep x2, DC in next 2sts, hdc in next 2sts, SC in next 5 sts, INC in next st, SC in next 5sts, hdc in next 2sts, DC in next 2sts,*(2DC in next st, DC in next 9sts)from*rep x2, 2DC in next st, sl st in 2nd Ch to join the round [67]
Rd 45	Ch2, DC in next 26sts, hdc in next 2sts, SC in next 5sts, **INC** in next st, SC in next 5sts, hdc in next 2sts, DC in next 26sts, sl st in 2nd Ch to join the round [69]
Rd 46	sl st in each st around [69]

Cut off **Bright Yellow**, weave in

STEP 2. BODY (work in continuous rounds)
When you change a yarn cut it off if it's stated in a pattern, in other cases, drop a yarn and raise when it's needed

Rd 1	**Dark Brown:** Hold the hat up-side-down. Start form the stitch with the marker of Rd 41: SC BLO in each st around [48] pic 1-2)

Rd 2	SC in next 20sts, SC BLO in next 8 sts (the beard will be attached to these sts), SC in next 20sts [48]

Rd 3	SC in each st around [48] Change to **Bright Yellow** in last st, do not cut off **Dark Brown**
Rd 4	**Bright Yellow:** SC in next 10sts, SC BLO in next 4 sts(the arm will be attached to these sts), SC in next 20sts, SC BLO in next 4sts(the arm will be attached to these sts), SC in next 10sts [48]
Rd 5-6	SC in each st around [48] Change to **Dark Brown** in last st
Rd 7-9	**Dark Brown:** SC in each st around [48] Change to **Bright Yellow** in last st

Rd 10	**Bright Yellow:** SC in each st around 48]
Rd 11	*(SC in next 7sts, INC in next st) from*rep x6 [54]
Rd 12	SC in each st around [54] Change to **Dark Brown** in last st
Rd 13	**Dark Brown:** SC in each st around [54]
Rd 14	*(SC in next 4sts, INC in next st, SC in next 4sts)from*rep x6 [60]
Rd 15	SC in each st around [60] Change to **Bright Yellow** in last st
Rd 16	**Bright Yellow:** SC in each st around [60]
Rd 17	*(SC in next 7sts, INC in next st, SC in next 7sts) from*rep x4 [64]
Rd 18	SC in each st around [64] Change to **Dark Brown** in last st. Cut off **Bright Yellow**
Rd 19	**Dark Brown:** SC in each st around [64]
Rd 20	*(SC in next 3sts, SC2tog, SC in next 3sts) from*rep x8 [56]
Rd 21-22	SC in each st around [56]
	Stuff
Rd 23	*(SC in next 5sts, SC2tog)from*rep x8 [48]
Rd 24-25	SC in each st around [48]
Rd 26	SC BLO in each st around [48]
Rd 27	SC in each st around [48]

Rd 28	*(SC in next 2sts, SC2tog, SC in next 2sts) from*rep x8 [40]
	Stuff
Rd 29	*(SC in next 3sts, SC2tog)from*rep x8 [32]
Rd 30	*(SC in next st, SC2tog, SC in next st) from*rep x8 [24]
Rd 31	*(SC in next st, SC2tog)from*rep x8 [16]
	Stuff
Rd 32	SC2tog x8 [8]

Cut off a thread. Sew the opening and weave in

ARMs (make x2, work in continuous rounds)

Rd 1	Honey caramel: 5SC in magic ring [5] tighten the ring
Rd 2	INC in each st around [10]
Rd 3-5	SC in each st around [10] Change to **Dark Brown** in last st. Cut off **Honey caramel**
Rd 6-17	**Dark Brown:** SC in each st around [10]

Cut off a thread, leaving a long tail for sewing

BEARD (work in continuous rounds)

Rd 1	White: 6SC in magic ring [6] tighten the ring
Rd 2	SC in each st around [6]
Rd 3	INC in each st around [12]
Rd 4	SC in next 2sts, INC in each of next 2sts, SC in next 4sts, INC in each of next 2sts, SC in next 2sts [16]
Rd 5	SC in next 3sts, INC in each of next 2sts, SC in next 6sts, INC in each of next 2sts, SC in next 3sts [20]
Rd 6	SC in next 4sts, INC in each of next 2sts, SC in next 8sts, INC in each of next 2sts, SC in next 4sts [24]
Rd 7	SC in next 5sts, INC in each of next 2sts, SC in next 10sts, INC in each of next 2sts, SC in next 5sts [28]
Rd 8	SC in next 6sts, INC in each of next 2sts, SC in next 12sts, INC in each of next 2sts, SC in next 6sts [32]
Rd 9-11	SC in each st around [32]
Rd 12	SC in next 6sts, SC2tog x2, SC in next 12sts, SC2tog x2, SC in next 6sts [28]
Rd 13	SC in next 5sts, SC2tog x2, SC in next 10sts, SC2tog x2, SC in next 5sts [24]
Rd 14	SC in next 4sts, SC2tog x2, SC in next 8sts, SC2tog x2, SC in next 4sts [20]
Rd 15	SC in next 3sts, SC2tog x2, SC in next 6sts, SC2tog x2, SC in next 3sts [16]

Cut off thread leaving a long tail for sewing

NOSE - USE **Honey caramel** COLOR AND REPEAT THE PATTERN FROM THE LADYBIRD PROJECT PAGE 44.

LEGS - USE **Bright Yellow** COLOR AND REPEAT THE PATTERN FROM THE LADYBIRD PROJECT PAGE 45.

FLOWERS PATTERS PAGE 15 – USE **White** FOR PETALS (MAKE 2) AND **Light Blue** FOR DISCS (MAKE 2)

WINGS – USE **White** COLOR AND REPEAT THE PATTERN FROM THE LADYBIRD PROJECT PAGE 46.

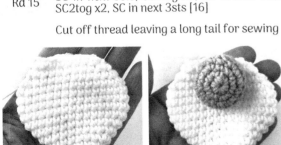

ASSEMBLING

1. Sew the nose on beard and then attach them on 8 stitches FLO of the body under the hat brim in front.

2. Sew the arms on 4 stitches FLO on Round 4 of the body under the hat brim on both sides.

3. Sew the wings on the body right behind the arms, making sure the top corner of the wings is connected to the Round 4. Securely attach only the top 4 stitches of the wings.

4. Sew the legs on the body Rd 25 stitches FLO.

5. Sew flowers on the hat.

Dandelion Gnome

SIZE: 30 cm / 12 in

	YARN BRAND AND COLORs		TOTAL FOR A PROJECT
Light Blue	⭐	Yarn Art Jeans 75	Approx. 20 g/70 meters
Brown	⭐	Yarn Art Jeans 40	Approx. 10 g/35 meters
Honey caramel	⭐	Yarn Art Jeans 07	Approx. 20 g/70 meters
Light Green	⭐	Yarn Art Jeans 29	Approx. 10 g/35 meters
Banana Yellow	⭐	Yarn Art Jeans 88	Approx. 5 g/20 meters

OTHER MATERIALS	CROCHET STICHES	TOOLS
Stuffing approx. 50 g	St(s), Ch, SC, hdc, INC, DC, TR, sl st, SC2tog, FLO, BLO, surface slip stitch	Crochet hook 2.5 mm Tapestry needle

Note: Make sure to use a contrasting thread to clearly mark the beginning of each round of your project. Don't remove the thread until your work is completed

HAT (work in continuous rounds)

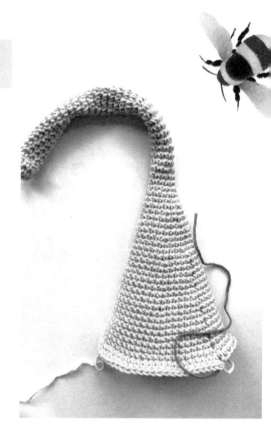

Rd 1	**Light Blue:** 6SC in magic ring [6] tighten the ring
Rd 2	*(INC in next st, SC in next st)from*rep x3 [9]
Rd 3-39	SC in each st around [9]
Rd 40	*(SC in next st, INC in next st, SC in next st) from*rep x3 [12]
Rd 41	SC in each st around [12]
Rd 42	*(SC in next 3sts, INC in next st)from*rep x3 [15]
Rd 43	SC in each st around [15]
Rd 44	*(SC in next 2sts, INC in next st, SC in next 2sts) from*rep x3 [18]
Rd 45	SC in each st around [18]
Rd 46	*(SC in next 5sts, INC in next st)from*rep x3 [21]
Rd 47	SC in each st around [21]
Rd 48	*(SC in next 3sts, INC in next st, SC in next 3sts) from*rep x3 [24]
Rd 49	SC in each st around [24]
Rd 50	*(SC in next 7sts, INC in next st)from*rep x3 [27]
Rd 51	SC in each st around [27]
Rd 52	*(SC in next 4sts, INC in next st, SC in next 4sts) from*rep x3 [30]
Rd 53	SC in each st around [30]
Rd 54	*(SC in next 9sts, INC in next st)from*rep x3 [33]
Rd 55	SC in each st around [33]
Rd 56	*(SC in next 5sts, INC in next st, SC in next 5sts) from*rep x3 [36]
Rd 57	SC in each st around [36]
Rd 58	*(SC in next 11sts, INC in next st)from*rep x3 [39]
Rd 59	SC in each st around [39]
Rd 60	*(SC in next 6sts, INC in next st, SC in next 6sts) from*rep x3 [42]
Rd 61	SC in each st around [42]
Rd 62	*(SC in next 13sts, INC in next st)from*rep x3 [45]

Rd 63	SC in each st around [45]
Rd 64	*(SC in next 7sts, INC in next st, SC in next 7sts) from*rep x3 [48]
Rd 65	SC in each st around [48]
Rd 66	*(SC in next 11sts, INC in next st)from*rep x4 [52]
Rd 67	SC in each st around [52]
Rd 68	*(SC FLO in next 6sts, INC FLO in next st, SC FLO in next 6sts)from*rep x4 [56]

Note: We will be working into these stitches BLO when we begin crocheting the body later on.

Rd 69	*(SC in next 13sts, INC in next st)from*rep x4 [60]
Rd 70	*(Ch1, skip next st, DC in next st, 3TR in next st, DC in next st, Ch1, skip next st, SC in next st)from*rep x10

Cut off **Light Blue**, weave in

BODY (work in continuous rounds)

Rd 1	Hold the hat upside-down, with **Honey caramel** work into stitches BLO of Rd 67: SC BLO in each st around [52]
Rd 2	SC in next 24sts, SC BLO in next 4sts (the nose will be attached to these sts), SC in next 24sts [52]
Rd 3	SC in each st around [52]
Rd 4	SC in next 11sts, SC BLO in next 4sts (the arm will be attached to these sts), SC in next 22sts, SC BLO in next 4sts (the arm will be attached to these sts), SC in next 11sts [52]
Rd 5 -7	SC in each st around [52]
Rd 8	*(SC in next 6sts, INC in next st, SC in next 6 sts) from*rep x4 [56]
Rd 9-10	SC in each st around [56]
Rd 11	*(SC in next 13sts, INC in next st) from*rep x4 [60]
Rd 12-14	SC in each st around [60]
Rd 15	*(SC in next 7sts, INC in next st, SC in next 7 sts) from*rep x4 [64]
Rd 16-17	SC in each st around[64] Change to **Brown** in last stitch. Cut off **Honey caramel**

Rd 18	**Brown:** *(SC BLO in next 3sts, SC2tog BLO, SC BLO in next 3sts)from*rep x8 [56]
Rd 19-20	SC in each st around [56]
	Drop a loop from your hook
	With **Light Blue:** work surface slip stitch into stitches of Rd 18. Cut off **Light Blue** (pic.2)
Rd 21	Grab a dropped **Brown** loop back on your hook and continue: *(SC in next 5sts, SC2tog)from*rep x8 [48]
	Stuff
Rd 22-23	SC in each st around [48]
Rd 24	SC BLO in each st around [48]
	Note: We will be working into these stitches FLO when we crocheting the stand later on
Rd 25	*(SC in next 2sts, SC2tog, SC in next 2sts) from*rep x8 [40]
Rd 26	*(SC in next 3sts, SC2tog)from*rep x8 [32]
Rd 27	*(SC in next st, SC2tog, SC in next st)from*rep x8 [24]
Rd 28	*(SC in next st, SC2tog)from*rep x8 [16]
	Stuff
Rd 29	SC2tog x8 [8]
	Cut off a thread and sew the opening, weave in

STAND

Rd 1	Hold the body upside-down. With **Light Blue** work into stitches FLO of Rd 23 of the Body: SC FLO in each st around [48] (pic.4) Cut off a thread and weave in

ARMs (make x2, work in continuous rounds)

STEP 1. ARM

Rd 1	**Banana Yellow:** 5SC in magic ring [5] tighten the ring
Rd 2	INC in each st around [10]
Rd 3-5	SC in each st around [10] Change to **Honey caramel** in last st. Cut off **Banana Yellow**
Rd 6-7	**Honey caramel:** SC in each st around [10]
Rd 8	SC BLO in each st around [10]
Rd 9-17	SC in each st around [10]

Cut off a thread, leaving a long tail for sewing.

STEP 2. CUFF

Rd 1	Hold the arm upside-down and work into stitches FLO of Rd 7 with **Light Blue:** SC FLO in each st around [10]
Rd 2	SC in each st around [10]

Cut off a thread and weave in

NOSE

Banana Yellow: make a pom-pom ⌀4cm

Cut off a thread, leaving a long tail for sewing

Make **SMALL LEAVES** x2 with **Light Green**. Find a photo tutorial and pattern on page 153.

Make **LARGE LEAF** x1 with **Light Green**. Find a photo tutorial and pattern on page 150.

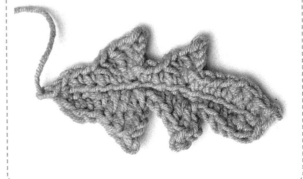

ASSEMBLING

1. Sew the arms to the stitches FLO of Rd 3 of the body on both sides.

2. To attach the leaves to the body, please arrange them as shown in the photo. Be sure to place them on the side of the body where you left 4 stitches FLO for the nose. Once you have them arranged, use a running stitch to attach them to the body securely.

3. With **Light Green** make several long stitches imitating a stem, and then attach the nose (pop-pom) to 4 stitches FLO under the hat brim.

4. Knot the hat.

5. Add an extra touch of style to your gnome's hat by making a **Brown** twisted cord (follow the instructions on the page 18)

Thistle Gnome

SIZE: 23 cm / 9 in

SAGE
32

	YARN BRAND AND COLORs	TOTAL FOR A PROJECT
Purple ★	Yarn Art Jeans 72	Approx. 25 g / 90 meters
Honey caramel ★	Yarn Art Jeans 07	Approx. 7 g / 20 meters
Grass Green ★	Yarn Art Jeans 69	Approx. 20 g / 70 meters
Light Green ★	Yarn Art Jeans 29	Approx. 3g

OTHER MATERIALS	CROCHET STICHES	TOOLS
Stuffing approx. 40 g	St(s), Ch, SC, hdc, DC, TR, INC, sl st, SC2tog, FLO, BLO	Crochet hook 2.5 mm Sewing needle

Note: Make sure to use a contrasting thread to clearly mark the beginning of each round of your project. Don't remove the thread until your work is completed.

STEP 1. HAT (work in continuous rounds)

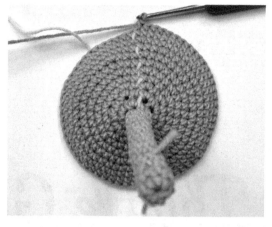

Rd 1	**Grass Green:** 6SC in magic ring [6] tighten the ring
Rd 2-17	SC in each st around [6]
Rd 18	SC in next 5 sts, INC in next st [7]
Rd 19	INC in each st around [14]
Rd 20	*(SC in next st, INC in next st)from*rep x7 [21]
Rd 21	*(SC in next st, INC in next st, SC in next st) from*rep x7 [28]
Rd 22	*(SC in next 3sts, INC in next st)from*rep x7 [35]
Rd 23	*(SC in next 2sts, INC in next st, SC in next 2sts) from*rep x7 [42]
Rd 24	*(SC in next 5sts, INC in next st)from*rep x7 [49]
Rd 25	*(SC in next 3sts, INC in next st, SC in next 3sts) from*rep x7 [56]
Rd 26	*(SC in next 7sts, INC in next st)from*rep x7 [63]
Rd 27-30	SC in each st around [63]
Rd 31	*(SC in next 19sts, SC2tog)from*rep x3 [60]
Rd 32	*(SC in next 9sts, SC2tog, SC in next 9sts) from*rep x3 [57]
Rd 33	*(SC in next 17sts, SC2tog)from*rep x3 [54]
Rd 34	*(SC in next 8sts, SC2tog, SC in next 8sts) from*rep x3 [51]
Rd 35	*(SC in next 15sts, SC2tog)from*rep x3 [48]
Rd 36	*(SC in next 7sts, SC2tog, SC in next 7sts) from*rep x3 [45]
Rd 37	*(SC in next 13sts, SC2tog)from*rep x3 [42]
Rd 38	*(SC in next 6sts, SC2tog, SC in next 6sts) from*rep x3 [39]
Rd 39	*(SC in next 11sts, SC2tog)from*rep x3 [36]
Rd 40	SC in each st around [36] Change to **Purple** in last st. Cut off **Grass Green**

Thistle Gnome

Rd 41   **Purple:** *(SC BLO in next 5sts, INC BLO in next st) from*rep x6 [42]

Note: To create the second layer of scallops on the hat, we will start crocheting into these stitches FLO later.

Rd 42   *(SC in next 3sts, INC in next st, SC in next 3sts) from*rep x6 [48]

Rd 43   SC FLO in each st around [48]

Note: To create the body, we will start crocheting into these stitches BLO later.

Rd 44   *(SC in next 7sts, INC in next st)from*rep x6 [54]

Rd 45   SC in each st around [54]

Rd 46   *(Ch3, sl st in 2nd st from hook, skip one stitch on a chain and one on the edge, sl st in next st of the edge)from*rep to end. Cut off **Purple** and weave in

STEP 2. BODY (work in continuous rounds)

Rd 1	Hold the hat upside-down and with **Purple** work into stitches BLO of Rd 42: SC BLO in each st around [48]
Rd 2	SC in next 20sts, SC BLO in next 8sts (the nose will be attached to these sts), SC in next 20sts [48]
Rd 3	SC in next 10sts, SC BLO in next 4sts(the arm will be attached to these sts), SC in next 20sts, SC BLO in next 4sts(the arm will be attached to these sts), SC in next 10sts [48]
Rd 4	SC in each st around [48]
Rd 5	(SC in next 11sts, INC in next st)from*rep x4 [52]
Rd 6	SC in each st around [52]
Rd 7	(SC in next 6sts, INC in next st, SC in next 6sts) from*rep x4 [56]
Rd 8-9	SC in each st around [56]
Rd 10	*(SC in next 3sts, INC in next st, SC in next 3sts) from*rep x8 [64]
Rd 11-13	SC in each st around [64]
Rd 14	*(SC in next 3sts, SC2tog, SC in next 3sts) from*rep x8 [56]
Rd 15-16	SC in each st around [56]
Rd 17	*(SC in next 5sts, SC2tog)from*rep x8 [48]
Rd 18-19	SC in each st around [48]
Rd 20	SC BLO in each st around [48]
Rd 21	*(SC in next 2sts, SC2tog, SC in next 2sts) from*rep x8 [40]
Rd 22	*(SC in next 3sts, SC2tog)from*rep x8 [32]
	Stuff
Rd 23	*(SC in next st, SC2tog, SC in next st) from*rep x8 [24]
Rd 24	*(SC in next st, SC2tog)from*rep x8 [16]
	Stuff
Rd 25	SC2tog x8 [8]
	Cut off a thread and sew the opening, weave in

Scallop layer on the hat
(work in continuous rounds)

Rd 1	**Purple:** Hold the body upside-down, join **Purple** and work into stitches FLO of Rd 40 of the hat (step 1): 2DC FLO in each st around
Rd 2	*(Ch2, sl st in next DC) from*rep around

Cut off **Purple** and weave in

ARMs (make x2, work in continuous rounds)

Rd 1	**Honey caramel:** 5SC in magic ring [5] Tighten the ring
Rd 2	INC in each st around [10]
Rd 3-4	SC in each st around [10] Change to **Grass Green** in last st.
	Cut off **Honey caramel**
Rd 5-6	**Grass Green:** SC in each st around [10]
Rd 7	SC BLO in each st around [10]
Rd 8-16	SC in each st around [10]
	Cut off a thread, leaving a long tail for sewing

CUFF

Rd 1	**Purple:** Hold the arm upside-down and work into stitches FLO of Rd 6: Ch1, *(hdc in next st, 2hdc in next st) from*rep around, sl st in 1st st of rd [15]
Rd 2	*(Ch2, sl st in next hdc)from*rep around
	Cut off **Purple**, weave in

BOOTS (work in continuous rounds)

Rd 1	**Purple:** 6SC in magic ring [6] Tighten the ring
Rd 2	INC in each st around [12]
Rd 3	*(SC in next st, INC in next st)from*rep x6 [18]
Rd 4-5	SC in each st around [18]
Rd 6	*(SC in next st, SC2tog)from*rep x6 [12]
	Now we need to stitch edges together. Stuff the boot a little amount of stuffing. Squeeze the opening and by SC stitch edges together inserting your hook through both layers (total is 6 SC)
	Cut off a thread, leaving a long tail for sewing

NOSE (work in continuous rounds)

Rd 1	**Honey caramel:** 6SC in magic ring [6] Tighten the ring
Rd 2	INC in each st around [12]
Rd 3	*(SC in next st, INC in next st)from*rep x6 [18]
Rd 4-5	SC in each st around [18]
Rd 6	*(SC in next st, SC2tog)from*rep x6 [12]
	Cut off a thread, leaving a long tail for sewing. Stuff the nose with a small amount of stuffing

Make **SMALL LEAVES** x2 with **Light Green**. Find a photo tutorial and pattern on page 153.

Make **LARGE LEAF** x1 with **Grass Green**. Find a photo tutorial and pattern on page 150.

ASSEMBLING

1. Sew arms on 4 stitches FLO of rd 2(body – STEP 2) on the sides under the hat brim.

2. Sew the nose and 2 **Light Green** leaves (imitate mustaches) on 8 stitches FLO of Rd 1 (body – STEP 2) in front of the body under the hat brim.

3. Sew the boots on the body Rd 19.

4. Attach large leaves to the stem of the hat.

Gnome- Bouquet

SIZE: 23 cm / 9 in

YARN BRAND AND COLORs		TOTAL FOR A PROJECT
Banana Yellow	Yarn Art Jeans 88	Approx. 15 g/45 meters
White	Yarn Art Jeans 62	Approx. 7 g/25 meters
Grass Green	Yarn Art Jeans 69	Approx. 7 g/25 meters
Honey caramel	Yarn Art Jeans 07	Approx. 5 g/20 meters
Blue	Yarn Art Jeans 76	Approx. 15 g/40 meters
Rose	Yarn Art Jeans 41	Approx. 10 g/35 meters
Yarn for flowers		
Light Blue	Yarn Art Jeans 75	Approx. 1 g
Black	Yarn Art Jeans 28	Approx. 1 g
Red	Yarn Art Jeans 90	Approx. 3 g
Light Green	Yarn Art Jeans 29	Approx. 1 g

OTHER MATERIALS	CROCHET STICHES	TOOLS
Stuffing approx. 40 g Cotton lace approx. 60 cm length	St(s), Ch, SC, hdc, DC, TR, INC, sl st, SC2tog, BPhdc, FLO, BLO	Crochet hook 2.5 mm Tapestry needle Stitch marker x2

Note: Make sure to use a contrasting thread to clearly mark the beginning of each round of your project. Don't remove the thread until your work is completed.

STEP 1. HAT (work in continuous rounds)

Rd 1	**Grass Green:** 6SC in magic ring [6] tighten the ring
Rd 2	INC in each st around [12]
Rd 3	*(SC in next st, INC in next st)from*rep x6 [18]
Rd 4	*(SC in next st, INC in next st, SC in next st) from*rep x6 [24]
Rd 5	*(SC in next 3sts, INC in next st) from*rep x6 [30]
Rd 6	BPhdc in each st around [30] Change to **Blue** in last st. Cut off **Grass Green** (pic. 1-2)
Rd 7-20	**Blue:** SC in each st around [30]
Rd 21	*(SC in next 9sts, INC in next st)from*rep x3 [33]
Rd 22	SC in each st around [33]
Rd 23	*(SC in next 5sts, INC in next st, SC in next 5sts) from*rep x3 [36]
Rd 24	SC in each st around [36]
Rd 25	*(SC in next 11sts, INC in next st)from*rep x3 [39]
Rd 26	SC in each st around [39]
Rd 27	*(SC in next 6sts, INC in next st, SC in next 6sts) from*rep x3 [42]
Rd 28	SC in each st around [42]
Rd 29	*(SC in next 13sts, INC in next st) from*rep x3 [45]
Rd 30	SC in each st around [45]
Rd 31	*(SC in next 7sts, INC in next st, SC in next 7sts) from*rep x3 [48]
Rd 32	SC in each st around [48] Mark this round by placing a stitch marker into the last st. In step 2, we will be attaching a hat brim with petals to these stitches BLO
Rd 33	*(SC FLO in next 5sts, INC FLO in next st) from*rep x8 [56]
Rd 34	*(SC in next 13sts, INC in next st) from*rep x4 [60]

| Rd 35 | *(SC in next 7sts, INC in next st, SC in next 7sts) from*rep x4 [64] |
| Rd 36 | sl st in in each st around [64] |

Cut off a thread and weave in

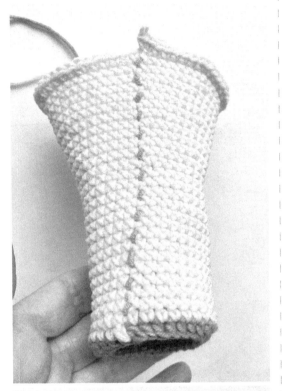

STEP 2. HAT BRIM (petal) (work in continuous rounds)

Rd 1	**Rose:** hold the hat upside-down and work in stitches BLO of Rd 32(the round marked by marker): SC BLO in each st around [48] Mark this round by placing a stitch marker into last stitch. In step 3, we will be attaching a hat brim with leaves to these stitches FLO
Rd 2	SC BLO in each st around [48]
Rd 3	*(SC in next 11 sts, INC in next st)from*rep x4 [52]
Rd 4	SC in each st around [52]

Place a stitch marker #2 into the last stitch of Rd 4, we will work the body into stitches of this round later

Rd 5	SC FLO in each st around [52]
Rd 6	*(SC in next 6sts, INC in next st, SC in next 6sts) from*rep x4 [56]
Rd 7	*(SC in next 13sts, INC in next st) from*rep x4 [60]
Rd 8	*(skip next 2sts, 6DC in next st, skip next 2sts, sl st in next st)from*rep x10 [10 shells]

Cut off a thread and weave in

STEP 3. HAT BRIM with LEAVES

Rd 1	**Grass Green:** hold the hat upside-down and work into stitches FLO of the marked round of Hat Brim with petals (step 2): *(skip next 2sts, 4DC FLO in next st, Ch2, sl st FLO in top of prev DC, 4DC FLO in same st as 4DC, skip next 2sts, sl st FLO in next st) from*rep x8 [8 shells] Cut off a thread and weave in

Sew the decorative cotton lace with a running stitch in between the hat brim and the leaf brim, gathering the lace as you go.

Crochet flowers (Poppy - page 81, Chamomile with **White+Light Blue** - page 15; Small **Rose** with **Banana Yellow** - page 17; Large **Rose** with **Rose** and x2 with **Banana Yellow** -page 17) and leaves with **Grass Green** (page 10). Finally, arrange the flowers and leaves onto your hat, making sure they sit between the hat brim with the petals and leaves, for a stunning finish.

BODY (work in continuous rounds)

Rd 1	**Banana Yellow:** hold the hat upside-down and work into stitches BLO of Rd 4 STEP 2 starting from the stitch marker #2: SC BLO in each st around [52]
Rd 2	SC in each st around [52]
Rd 3	SC in next 22sts, SC BLO in next 8sts(we will attach a nose and a beard to these sts), SC in next 22sts [52]
Rd 4	SC in next 11sts, SC BLO in next 4sts(we will attach an arm to these sts), SC in next 22sts, SC BLO in next 4sts(we will attach an arm to these sts), SC in next 11sts [52]
Rd 5-7	SC in each st around [52]
Rd 8	*(SC in next 6sts, INC in next st, SC in next 6sts) from*rep x4 [56]
Rd 9-10	SC in each st around [56]
Rd 11	*(SC in next 13sts, INC in next st)from*rep x4 [60]
Rd 12-14	SC in each st around [60]
Rd 15	*(SC in next 7sts, INC in next st, SC in next 7sts) from*rep x4 [64]
Rd 16-17	SC in each st around [64] Change to **Blue** in last st. Cut off Banana yellow
Rd 18	**Blue:** *(SC BLO in next 3sts, SC2tog BLO, SC BLO in next 3sts)from*rep x8 [56]
Rd 19-20	SC in each st around [56]
Rd 21	*(SC in next 5sts, SC2tog)from*rep x8 [48]
	Stuff
Rd 22-23	SC in each st around [48]
Rd 24	SC BLO in each st around [48]
Rd 25	*(SC in next 2sts, SC2tog, SC in next 2sts) from*rep x8 [40]
Rd 26	*(SC in next 3sts, SC2tog)from*rep x8 [32]
Rd 27	*(SC in next st, SC2tog, SC in next st)from*rep x8 [24]
Rd 28	*(SC in next st, SC2tog)from*rep x8 [16]
	Stuff
Rd 29	SC2tog x8 [8]

Cut off a thread and sew the opening, weave in

STAND

Grass Green: hold the body up-side-down and work in stitches FLO of Rd 23 of the body: SC FLO in each st around [48] Cut off a thread and weave in

| Rd 1 | |

Make a twisted cord (see page 18) with **Rose** yarn. Tie the hat.

ARMs (make x2, work in continuous rounds)

STEP 1. ARM

Rd 1	**Honey caramel:** 5SC in magic ring [5] Tighten the ring
Rd 2	INC in each st around [10]
Rd 3-5	SC in each st around [10] Change to **Banana Yellow** in last st. Cut off **Honey caramel**
Rd 6-7	**Banana Yellow:** SC in each st around [10]
Rd 8	SC BLO in each st around [10]
Rd 9-17	SC in each st around [10]

Cut off a thread, leaving a long tail for sewing

STEP 2. CUFF

Rd 1	**Blue:** Hold the arm upside-down and work in stitches FLO of Rd 7: SC FLO in each st around [10]
Rd 2	SC in each st around [10]

Cut off a thread and weave in

BEARD (work in continuous rounds)

White: Chain 2 [2]

Rd 1   3SC in 2nd st from hook [3] (work in continuous rounds)

Rd 2   INC in each of next 3SC [6]

Rd 3   INC in each of next 2sts, SC in next 2sts, INC in next st, SC in next st [9]

Rd 4   SC in next st, INC in each of next 2sts, SC in next 5sts, INC in next st [12]

Rd 5   SC in next 2sts, INC in each of next 2sts, SC in next 5sts, INC in next st, SC in next 2sts [15]

Rd 6   SC in next 3sts, INC in each of next 2sts, SC in next 9sts, INC in next st [18]

Rd 7   SC in next 4sts, INC in each of next 2sts, SC in next 8sts, INC in next st, SC in next 3sts [21]

Rd 8   SC in next 5sts, INC in each of next 2sts, SC in next 14sts [23]

Rd 9   SC in next 6sts, INC in each of next 2sts, SC in next 14sts, INC in next st [26]

Rd 10-12   SC in each st around [26]

Rd 13   SC in next 8sts, SC2tog, SC in next 11sts, SC2tog, SC in next 3sts [24]

Rd 14   SC in next 7sts, SC2tog, SC in next 10sts, SC2tog, SC in next 3sts [22]

Rd 15   SC in next 6sts, SC2tog, SC in next 9sts, SC2tog, SC in next 3sts [20]

Cut off a thread, leaving a long tail for sewing

NOSE (work in continuous rounds)

Rd 1	Honey caramel: 6SC in magic ring [6] Tighten the ring
Rd 2	INC in each st around [12]
Rd 3	*(SC in next st, INC in next st)from*rep x6 [18]
Rd 4-5	SC in each st around [18]
Rd 6	*(SC in next st, SC2tog)from*rep x6 [12]

Cut off a thread, leaving a long tail for sewing. Stuff the nose with a small amount of stuffing

ASSEMBLING

1. Sew the nose on the beard and sew all together on 8 stitches FLO the body under the hat brim.
2. Attach the arms to 4 stitches FLO of the body on both sides.

Sunflower Gentleman

SIZE: 22 cm / 8 in

YARN BRAND AND COLORs			TOTAL FOR A PROJECT
Off-White	☆	Yarn Art Jeans 03	Approx. 20g/70 meters
Honey caramel	★	Yarn Art Jeans 07	Approx. 5g/15 meters
Light Green	★	Yarn Art Jeans 29	Approx. 25 g/80 meters
Bright Yellow	★	Yarn Art Jeans 35	Approx. 3g/15 meters
Brown	★	Yarn Art Jeans 40	Approx. 6g/20 meters
Dark Green	★	Yarn Art Jeans 82	Approx. 3 g/10 meters
Dark Brown	★	Yarn Art Jeans 70	Approx. 1g(for a cord)

OTHER MATERIALS	CROCHET STICHES	TOOLS
Stuffing approx. 50 g	St(s), Ch, SC, hdc, DC, TR, INC, sl st, SC2tog, FLO, BLO	Crochet hook 2.5 mm Tapestry needle

Note: Make sure to use a contrasting thread to clearly mark the beginning of each round of your project. Don't remove the thread until your work is completed.

STEP 1. HAT (work in continuous rounds)

Rd 1	**Light Green:** 6SC in magic ring [6] tighten the ring
Rd 2-7	SC in each st around [6]
Rd 8	*(SC in next st, INC in next st)from*rep x3 [9]
Rd 9-12	SC in each st around [9]
Rd 13	*(SC in next st, INC in next st, SC in next st) from*rep x3 [12]
Rd 14-16	SC in each st around [12]
Rd 17	*(SC in next 3sts, INC in next st)from*rep x3 [15]
Rd 18-20	SC in each st around [15]

To gather your crocheted hat, follow this simple trick: Use a yarn of a different color from your hat and tie a knot. Place the knot on the wrong side of the hat and use this thread to mark the beginning of each round (as shown in the image with the **Brown** thread). Once you've completed the hat, gently pull on this thread to gather the hat and achieve the perfect shape.

Rd 21	*(SC in next 2sts, INC in next st, SC in next 2sts) from*rep x3 [18]
Rd 22-24	SC in each st around [18]
Rd 25	*(SC in next 5sts, INC in next st)from*rep x3 [21]
Rd 26-28	SC in each st around [21]
Rd 29	*(SC in next 3sts, INC in next st, SC in next 3sts) from*rep x3 [24]
Rd 30-32	SC in each st around [24]
Rd 33	*(SC in next 7sts, INC in next st)from*rep x3 [27]
Rd 34-36	SC in each st around [27]
Rd 37	*(SC in next 4sts, INC in next st, SC in next 4sts) from*rep x3 [30]
Rd 38-40	SC in each st around [30]
Rd 41	*(SC in next 9sts, INC in next st)from*rep x3 [33]
Rd 42-44	SC in each st around [33]
Rd 45	*(SC in next 5sts, INC in next st, SC in next 5sts) from*rep x3 [36]
Rd 46-48	SC in each st around [36]
Rd 49	*(SC in next 11sts, INC in next st)from*rep x3 [39]

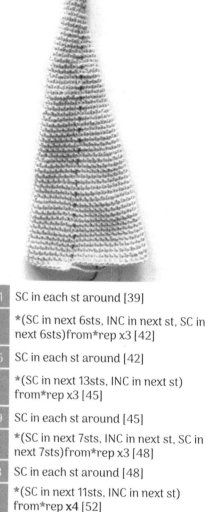

Rd 50-51	SC in each st around [39]
Rd 52	*(SC in next 6sts, INC in next st, SC in next 6sts)from*rep x3 [42]
Rd 53-55	SC in each st around [42]
Rd 56	*(SC in next 13sts, INC in next st) from*rep x3 [45]
Rd 57-59	SC in each st around [45]
Rd 60	*(SC in next 7sts, INC in next st, SC in next 7sts)from*rep x3 [48]
Rd 61-63	SC in each st around [48]
Rd 64	*(SC in next 11sts, INC in next st) from*rep **x4** [52]
Rd 64-66	SC in each st around [52]
Rd 67	*(SC in next 6sts, INC in next st, SC in next 6sts)from*rep x4 [56]
Rd 68-70	SC in each st around [56]

To gather the hat, simply pull the thread and secure it in place. If you haven't already placed a thread, you can achieve the same result by sewing the hat with a running stitch and pulling it tight.

STEP 2. Continue - HAT BRIM (work in continuous rounds)

Rd 71	*(SC FLO in next 13sts, INC FLO in next st) from*rep x4 [60]
Rd 72	*(SC in next 9sts, INC in next st)from*rep x6 [66]
Rd 73	*(SC in next 5sts, INC in next st, SC in next 5sts) from*rep x6 [72]
Rd 74	*(SC in next 11sts, INC in next st)from*rep x6 [78]
Rd 75	slip stitch in each st around [78]
	Cut off a thread and wave in

STEP 3. BODY (work in continuous rounds)

Rd 1	**Off-White:** Hold the hat upside-down. Work into stitches BLO of Rd 70, starting from the first stitch of the round: SC BLO in each st around [56]
Rd 2	SC in next 10sts, SC BLO in next 4 sts(the arm will be attached to these sts), SC in next 9 sts, SC BLO in next 10sts(the beard with nose will be attached to these sts), SC in next 9sts , SC BLO in next 4 sts(the arm will be attached to these sts), SC in next 10 sts [56]
Rd 3-6	SC in each st around [56]
Rd 7	*(SC in next 13sts, INC in next st) from*rep x4 [60]
Rd 8-11	SC in each st around [60]
Rd 12	*(SC in next 7sts, INC in next st, SC in next 7sts) from*rep x4 [64]
Rd 13-14	SC in each st around [64]
Rd 15	*(SC in next 3sts, SC2tog, SC in next 3sts) from*rep x8 [56]
Rd 16-18	SC in each st around [56] Stuff
Rd 19	*(SC in next 5sts, SC2tog)from*rep x8 [48]
Rd 20-21	SC in each st around [48]
Rd 22	SC BLO in each st around [48]
Rd 23	*(SC in next 2sts, SC2tog, SC in next 2sts) from*rep x8 [40]
Rd 24	*(SC in next 3sts, SC2tog)from*rep x8 [32]
Rd 25	*(SC in next st, SC2tog, SC in next st)from*rep x8 [24]
Rd 26	*(SC in next st, SC2tog)from*rep x8 [16] Stuff
Rd 27	SC2tog x8 [8] Cut off a thread and sew the opening, weave in

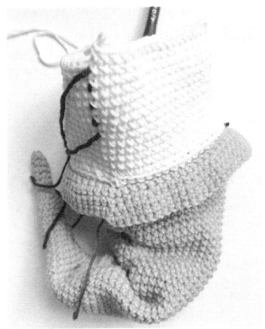

STEP 4. STAND

Rd 1	Hold the body upside-down. With **Light Green** work into stitches of Rd 21 of the body: SC FLO in each st around. [48]

Cut off a thread and weave in

NOSE (work in continuous rounds)

Rd 1	**Honey caramel:** 6SC in magic ring [6] tighten the ring
Rd 2	INC in each st around [12]
Rd 3	*(SC in next st, INC in next st)from*rep x6 [18]
Rd 4	*(SC in next 2sts, INC in next st)from*rep x6 [24]
Rd 5-6	SC in each st around [24]
Rd 7	*(SC in next st, SC2tog)from*rep x8 [16]
Rd 8	SC in each st around [16]

Cut off a thread, leaving a long tail for sewing. Stuff the nose with a small amount of stuffing

ARMs (make x2, work in continuous rounds)

STEP 1. ARM

Rd 1	**Honey caramel:** 5SC in magic ring [5] tighten the ring
Rd 2	INC in each st around [10]
Rd 3-5	SC in each st around. Change to **Off-White** in last st [10]

Cut off **Honey caramel**

Rd 6-7	**Off-White:** SC in each st around [10]
Rd 8	SC BLO in each st around [10]
Rd 9-17	SC in each st around [10]

Cut off a thread, leave a lonf tail for sewing

STEP 2. CUFF (work in continuous rounds)

Rd 1	Hold the arm upside-down and with **Light Green** work into stitches of Rd 7: SC FLO in each st around [10]
Rd 2-3	SC in each st around [10]

Cut off a thread and weave in

BEARD (work in continuous rounds)

	Brown: Chain 2
Rd 1	3SC in in 2nd st from hook [3] (work in round)
Rd 2	INC in each of next 3SC [6]
Rd 3	INC in each of next 2sts, SC in next 2sts, INC in next st, SC in next st [9]
Rd 4	SC in next st, INC in each of next 2sts, SC in next 5sts, INC in next st [12]
Rd 5	SC in next 2sts, INC in each of next 2sts, SC in next 5sts, INC in next st, SC in next 2sts [15]
Rd 6	SC in next 3sts, INC in each of next 2sts, SC in next 9sts, INC in next st [18]
Rd 7	SC in next 4sts, INC in each of next 2sts, SC in next 8sts, INC in next st, SC in next 3sts [21]
Rd 8	SC in next 5sts, INC in each of next 2sts, SC in next 14sts [23]
Rd 9	SC in next 6sts, INC in each of next 2sts, SC in next 14sts, INC in next st [26]

Rd 10-11	SC in each st around [26]
Rd 12	SC in next 7sts, INC in each of next 2sts, SC in next 14sts, INC in next st, SC in next 2sts [29]
Rd 13	SC in each st around [29]
Rd 14	SC in next 8sts, INC in each of next 2sts, SC in next 14sts, INC in next st, SC in next 4sts [32]
Rd 15	SC in each st around [32]
Rd 16	SC in next 9sts, INC in each of next 2sts, SC in next 21 sts [34]
Rd 17	SC in each st around [34]
Rd 18	SC in next 10sts, INC in each of next 2sts, SC in next 16sts, INC in next st, SC in next 5sts [37]
Rd 19-20	SC in each st around [37]

Cut off a thread. Sew or glue the nose on the beard

125

ASSEMBLING

1. Attach the beard with the nose to 10 stitches FLO of the body under the hat brim in front.

2. Sew the arms on 4 stitches FLO of the body on both sides.

3. Tie the twisted cord around the hat and sew or glue the sunflower on the hat.

Crochet Sunflower - see page 70.

Make a twisted cord with Dark Brown - page 18.

Lady Sunflower Gnome

SIZE: 25 cm / 10 in
LEVEL: EXPERIENCED

YARN BRAND AND COLORs		TOTAL FOR A PROJECT
Off-White	Yarn Art Jeans 03	Approx. 20 g/70 meters
Dark Brown ★	Yarn Art Jeans 70	Approx. 10 g/35 meters
Honey caramel ★	Yarn Art Jeans 07	Approx. 5 g/15 meters
Light Green ★	Yarn Art Jeans 29	Approx. 10 g/35 meters
Bright Yellow ★	Yarn Art Jeans 35	Approx. 15 g/50 meters
Brown ★	Yarn Art Jeans 40	Approx. 1g

OTHER MATERIALS	CROCHET STICHES	TOOLS
Stuffing approx. 50 g	St(s), Ch, SC, hdc, DC, INC, sl st, SC2tog, FLO, BLO, surface(flat)slip stitch	Crochet hook 2.5 mm Tapestry needle Stitch marker

STEP 1.
Make 5 squares

Each square is made up of 3 colors, and measures approx. 5 cm × 5 cm

Rd 1

Dark Brown: work in magic ring: Ch2, 11DC, sl st in Ch 2nd st of rd [12]. Tighten the ring
Cut off a thread and weave in

Round with Petals:

Rd 2

Join **Bright Yellow:**

1) Chain 3 (count as 1 DC)

2) **PETAL: 4DC in next st

3) Drop a loop from your hook

4) Inset a hook into 3rd Chain. When you will wok other petals insert your hook in 1st DC

5) And insert the hook back into the dropped loop

6) Yarn over and pull through both loops on your hook. Petal is done.

Now work:
(Ch2, Petal** in next st) repeat this pattern around, and work sl st in 3rd ch in the end of rd (total is 12 petals).
Cut off a thread
Result - Pic.2-3 below

Rd 3

Now Join **Light Green** to beginning of rd and work(pic.4): Ch1, *(SC in next st, 2SC in next 2Ch-space, SC in next st, 2SC in next 2Ch-space, SC in next st, SC in next 2Ch-space)from*rep x4, sl st in 1st st of rd(don't count as st). Total is 32 stitches

Rd 4

Ch3, *(DC+hdc in next st, SC in next 6sts, hdc+DC in next st)from*rep x3, DC+hdc in next st, SC in next 6sts, hdc in next st, sl st in 3rd Ch(don't count as st). Total is 40 sts. Cut off a thread.Result - pic.1

Watch Video-Granny square Row 3-4

STEP 2. Decorating and JOINING.

We are going to use a flat(surface) slip stitch back loops only and **Off-White** to join all squares together and decorate the rest of sides.

1. A principal of joining: Join 2 squares working flat slip stitch in each stitch between square's corners(chains) across the side edge inserting your hook through both squares back loops only (we work 10 slip stitches in total on each side.

2. When you have finished joining all squares together, you need to join the last square to the first square to make "a tube".

3. To decorate the rest of edges, join a thread to the sides that must be decorated, work flat slip stitches BLO and fasten off.

Result

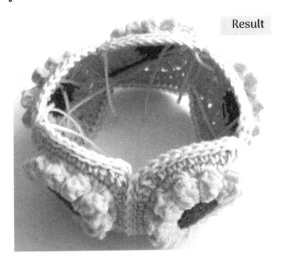

STEP 3. HAT (work in continuous rounds)

To ensure that you don't miss any stitch while working on a project, it's recommended to use a contrast thread at the beginning of each round. This thread should remain in place until the item is completed.

Rd 1	**Off-White:** 6SC in magic ring [6] tighten the ring	Rd 10	*(SC in next 3sts, INC in next st)from*rep x4 [20]
Rd 2	SC in each st around [6]	Rd 11-12	SC in each st around [20]
Rd 3	*(SC in next st, INC in next st)from*rep x3 [9]		
Rd 4	SC in each st around [9]	Rd 13	*(SC in next 2sts, INC in next st, SC in next 2sts) from*rep x4 [24]
Rd 5	*(SC in next st, INC in next st, SC in next st) from*rep x3 [12]	Rd 14-15	SC in each st around [24]
Rd 6	SC in each st around [12]		
Rd 7	*(SC in next st, INC in next st, SC in next st) from*rep **x4** [16]	Rd 16	*(SC in next 5sts, INC in next st)from*rep x4 [28]
Rd 8-9	SC in each st around [16]	Rd 17-18	SC in each st around [28]

131

Rd 19	*(SC in next 3sts, INC in next st, SC in next 3sts) from*rep x4 [32]
Rd 20-21	SC in each st around [32]
Rd 22	*(SC in next 7sts, INC in next st) from*rep x4 [36]
Rd 23-24	SC in each st around [36]
Rd 25	*(SC in next 4sts, INC in next st, SC in next 4sts) from*rep x4 [40]
Rd 26-27	SC in each st around [40]
Rd 28	*(SC in next 9sts, INC in next st)from*rep x4 [44]
Rd 29-30	SC in each st around [44]. Change to **Dark Brown** in last st. Leave **Off-White** on a wrong side
Rd 31	**Dark Brown:** *(SC in next 5sts, INC in next st, SC in next 5sts)from*rep x4 [48]
Rd 32	SC in each st around [48]. Change to **Bright Yellow** in last st.
	Cut off **Dark Brown**
Rd 33	**Bright Yellow:** SC in each st around [48]
Rd 34	*(SC in next 11sts, INC in next st)from*rep x4 [52]
	Change to **Light Green** in last st. Cut off **Bright Yellow**
Rd 35-36	**Light Green:** SC in each st around [52] Change to **Off-White**. Cut off **Light Green**
Rd 37	**Off-White:** *(SC in next 8sts, INC in next st, SC in next 8sts)from*rep x3, SC in next st [55]
Rd 38	SC in each st around [55] Place a stitch marker into last st
Rd 39-40	SC BLO in each st around [55]
Rd 41-45	SC in each st around [55]
	Cut off a thread leaving a long tail for sewing

STEP 4. JOIN CONE AND TUBE.

Join edge stitches of the tube and the cone together by the tapestry needle and **Off-White** thread.

To join the cone and tube together, we'll need to stitch 55 stitches for the cone and 50 stitches for the tube, one by one. We'll add one additional stitch in between each two squares(it's going to be 5 additional stitches). By doing so, we'll be able to match the number of stitches on the edges of both details.

STEP 5. BODY BOTTOM

Rd 1 — Grab the cone upside-down, right side facing. Join **Off-White** to beginning of rd and work SC in each stitch of each square (each square consists of 10 stitches) and + 1 SC in between each 2 squares [total is 55 stitches]

Rd 2 — INC in next st, SC in each st around [56]

Rd 3 — *(SC in next 5sts, SC-2tog)from*rep x8 [48]

Stuff as you go

Rd 4 — SC BLO in each st around [48]

Rd 5 — *(SC in next 2sts, SC-2tog, SC in next 2sts) from*rep x8 [40]

Rd 6 — *(SC in next 3sts, SC-2tog)from*rep x8 [32]

Rd 7 — *(SC in next st, SC2tog, SC in next st)from*rep x8 [24]

Rd 8 — *(SC in next st, SC2tog) from*rep x8 [16] Stuff

Rd 9 — SC2tog x8 [8]

Cut off a thread and sew the opening, weave in

STEP 6. HAT BRIM - LEAVES

Rd 1 — Hold the item ipside-down and with **Light Green** work into stitches FLO of 38th rd of the hat, starting from the stitch marker: INC FLO in nexr st, SC FLO in each st around [56]

Rd 2 — *(skip next st, 3DC in next st, Ch3, slip stitch in top of prev DC, 3DC in same stitch as prev 3DC, skip next st, sl st in next st)from*rep x14.

Total is 14 shells. Cut off a thread and weave in

ARMs (make x2) (work in continuous rounds)

Rd 1	**Honey caramel:** 5SC in magic ring [5] tighten the ring
Rd 2	INC in each st around [10]
Rd 3-5	SC in each st around [10] Change to Off-White in last t. Cut off **Honey caramel**
Rd 6-17	**Off-White:** SC in each st around [10]

Cut off a thread, leaving a long tail for sewing

NOSE (work in continuous rounds)

Rd 1	**Honey caramel:** 6SC in magic ring [6] tighten the ring
Rd 2	INC in each st around [12]
Rd 3	*(SC in next st, INC in next st)from*rep x6 [18]
Rd 4-5	SC in each st around [18]
Rd 6	*(SC in next st, SC2tog)from*rep x6 [12]

Cut off a thread, leaving a long tail for sewing. Stuff the nose with a small amount of stuffing

Make a twisted cord with Dark green (page 18) and decorate the hat.

Sew or glue the nose on the body.

Sew the arms on the body.

Sunflower Pin Cushion

SIZE: 8 cm / 3.5 in

YARN BRAND AND COLORs			TOTAL FOR A PROJECT
Off-White	☆	Yarn Art Jeans 03	Approx. 10 g/35 meters
Dark Brown	★	Yarn Art Jeans 70	Approx. 10 g/35 meters
Honey caramel	★	Yarn Art Jeans 07	Approx. 7 g/10 meters
Light Green	★	Yarn Art Jeans 29	Approx. 10 g/35 meters
Bright Yellow	★	Yarn Art Jeans 35	Approx. 10 g/35 meters
Brown	★	Yarn Art Jeans 40	Approx. 5 g/17 meters
Dark Green	★	Yarn Art Jeans 82	Approx. 1g

OTHER MATERIALS	CROCHET STICHES	TOOLS
Stuffing approx. 20 g	St(s), Ch, SC, hdc, DC, TR, INC, sl st, SC2tog, FLO, BLO, surface slip stitch	Crochet hook 2.5 mm Tapestry needle

HAT

Note: Make sure to use a contrasting thread to clearly mark the beginning of each round of your project. Don't remove the thread until your work is completed

HAT + BODY (work in continuous rounds)

Rd 1	**Dark Brown:** 6SC in magic ring [6]tighten the ring
Rd 2	INC in next 6 sts [12]
Rd 3	*(SC in next st, INC in next st)from*rep x6 [18]
Rd 4	*(SC in next st, INC in next st, SC in next st) from*rep x6 [24]
Rd 5	*(SC in next 3sts, INC in next st)from*rep x6 [30]
Rd 6	*(SC in next 2sts, INC in next st, SC in next 2sts) from*rep x6 [36]
Rd 7	*(SC in next 5sts, INC in next st)from*rep x6 [42]
Rd 8	*(SC in next 3sts, INC in next st, SC in next 3sts) from*rep x6 [48]
Rd 9	*(SC in next 7sts, INC in next st)from*rep x6 [54]
Rd 10-13	SC in each st around [54]
Rd 14	*(SC BLO in next 8sts, SC2tog BLO, SC BLO in next 8sts)from*rep x3 [51]
Rd 15	*(SC in next 15sts, SC2tog)from*rep x3 [48]
	Cut off a thread
Rd 16	Join **Light Green:** SC BLO in each st around [48]
	Cut off a thread and weave in

Scan for the video tutorial – How to crochet Petals

Continue – Petal:

Join **Bright Yellow** to Rd 13 and work into stitches FLO: Chain 3 (count as 1 DC) pic.3, **PETAL:** 4DC in next st pic.4; Drop a loop from your hook pic.5; Inset a hook into 3rd Chain (for other petals insert your hook in 1st DC) pic.6; Insert the hook back into the dropped loop pic.7; Yarn over and pull through both loops on your hook pic.8. Petal is done. Then work to end: (Ch2, skip next stitch, work Petal in next st), and sl st at the end to join the round. Cut off a thread

Rd 17	Join **Off-White**: SC BLO in each st around [48]
Rd 18-19	SC in each st around [48]
Rd 20	*(SC in next 11sts, INC in next st)from*rep x4 [52]
Rd 21-22	SC in each st around [52]
Rd 23	*(SC in next 6sts, INC in next st, SC in next 6sts) from*rep x4 [56]
Rd 24-26	SC in each st around [56]Change to **Light green** in last st. Cut off a thread
Rd 27	**Light Green:** *(SC BLO in next 5sts, SC2tog BLO) from*rep x8 [48]
Rd 28-29	SC in each st around [48]
Rd 30	SC BLO in each st around [48]
	Drop the loop from your hook
	Decorate the body with **Dark Green**: surface slip stitch into stitches of Rd 27. Cut off a thread (pic. 2) weave in
Rd 31	Grab a dropped loop and continue working: *(SC in next 2sts, SC2tog, SC in next 2sts) from*rep x8 [40]
	Stuff
Rd 32	*(SC in next 3sts, SC2tog)from*rep x8 [32]
Rd 33	*(SC in next st, SC2tog, SC in next st) from*rep x8 [24]
Rd 34	*(SC in next st, SC2tog) from*rep x8 [16]
	Stuff well
Rd 35	SC2tog x8 [8]
	Cut off a thread and sew the opening

STEP 2. LEAVES

Rd 1	With a new **Light Green** work into stitch FLO of 15th rd of the hat(step 1): SC FLO in each st around [48]
Rd 2	*(skip next 2sts, [3DC, TR] all in next stitch, Ch4, slip stitch in top of prev TR, [TR, 3DC] in same stitch as prev [3DC, TR], skip next 2sts, sl st in next st)from*rep x8. Total is 8 leaves

Cut off a thread and weave in

STEP 3. STAND

Rd 1	Hold the item upside-down, with **Dark Brown** work into stitch FLO of Rd 29 of the body(-step 1), starting from the beginning of rd: SC FLO in each st around [48]

Cut off a thread and weave in

ARMs (make x2) (work in continuous rounds)

Rd 1	**Honey caramel:** 5SC in magic ring [5] tighten the ring
Rd 2	INC in each st around [10]
Rd 3-4	SC in each st around [10]Change to **Off-White** in last st. Cut off **Honey caramel**
Rd 5-6	**Off-White:** SC in each st around [10]
Rd 7	SC BLO in each st around [10]
Rd 8-12	SC in each st around [10]

Cut off a thread, leaving a long tail for sewing

NOSE (work in continuous rounds)

Rd 1	**Honey caramel:** 6SC in magic ring [6] tighten the ring
Rd 2	INC in each st around [12]
Rd 3	*(SC in next st, INC in next st)from*rep x6 [18]
Rd 4-5	SC in each st around [18]
Rd 6	*(SC in next st, SC2tog)from*rep x6 [12]

Cut off a thread, leaving a long tail for sewing. Stuff the nose

BEARD (work in continuous rounds)

	Brown: Chain 2 [2]
Rd 1	3SC in in 2nd st from hook [3]
Rd 2	INC in each of next 3SC [6]
Rd 3	INC in each of next 2sts, SC in next 2sts, INC in next st, SC in next st [9]
Rd 4	SC in next st, INC in each of next 2sts, SC in next 5sts, INC in next st [12]
Rd 5	SC in next 2sts, INC in each of next 2sts, SC in next 5sts, INC in next st, SC in next 2sts [15]
Rd 6	SC in next 3sts, INC in each of next 2sts, SC in next 9sts, INC in next st [18]
Rd 7	SC in next 4sts, INC in each of next 2sts, SC in next 8sts, INC in next st, SC in next 3sts [21]
Rd 8	SC in next 5sts, INC in each of next 2sts, SC in next 14sts [23]
Rd 9	SC in each st around [23]
Rd 10	SC in next 5sts, SC2tog, SC in next 9sts, SC2tog, SC in next 5sts [21]
Rd 11	SC in next 4sts, SC2tog, SC in next 9sts, SC2tog, SC in next 4sts [19]. Cut off a thread, leaving a long tail for sewing

ASSEMBLING

1. Sew or glue the nose on the beard, then attach them to stitches FLO of Rd 1 of the body, making sure the nose sits in between two leaves for a cute look.
2. Sew the arms to stitches FLO of Rd 1 of the body under the leaves.

Wellington and Tulips

SIZE OF THE BOOT: 9 cm / 3.5 in

	YARN BRAND AND COLORs		TOTAL FOR 1 BOOT AND 1 TULIP
Jeans Blue	★	Yarn Art Jeans 68	Approx. 10 g/35 meters
Bright Yellow	★	Yarn Art Jeans 35	Approx. 15 g/50 meters
Red	★	Yarn Art Jeans 90	Approx. 15 g/50 meters
Grass Green	★	Yarn Art Jeans 69	Approx. 5 g/15 meters

OTHER MATERIALS	CROCHET STICHES	TOOLS
• Stuffing approx. 5 • Dowel Rods Wood Sticks (1/8inch or 3mm) • A bit of Black or Brown yarn to embroider a clasp	St(s), Ch, SC, hdc, INC, sl st, SC2tog, FLO, BLO, surface slip stitch	Crochet hook 2.5 mm Tapestry needle Stitch marker ×1

WELLINGTON

Note: Make sure to use a contrasting thread to clearly mark the beginning of each round of your project. Don't remove the thread until your work is completed.

STEP 1. SOLE (work in continuous round) make x2

	Jeans Blue: Foundation chain: Chain 9
Rd 1	INC into 2nd st from hook, SC in next 4 sts, hdc in next 2 sts, 8hdc in last st of foundation chain, work in other side of a foundation chain: hdc in next 2sts, SC in next 4 sts, INC in the same stitch as the first INC in this round [24]
Rd 2	INC in each of next 2 sts, SC in next 7 sts, INC in each of next 6 sts, SC in next 7 sts, INC in each of next 2 sts [34]
Rd 3	SC in next 2 sts, INC in next st, SC in next 10 sts, INC in each of next 2 sts, SC in next 4sts, INC in each of next next 2 sts, SC in next 10 sts, INC in next st, SC in next 2 sts [40]

Cut off a thread. Weave in (watch the video tutorial for an invisible finish - see page 9). Pic.1. Make x2 soles.

STEP 2. HEEL

Row 1	5SC in magic ring[5] tighten the ring. Turn
Row 2	Ch1, *(INC in next st, SC in next st)from*rep x2, INC in next st[8] Turn
Rd 3	Ch1, SC in next st, INC in next st, SC in next 4 sts, INC in next st, SC in next st, continue on the straight edge and work 1SC in each row (total is 7 SC) Cut off and weave in. Pic.2

Stitch one sole with the heel.

Grab one sole and place the wrong side of the heel piece on the right side of the sole on the narrow side(pic.3). Using **Jeans Blue** thread, stitch the two pieces together with slip stitches, working through the edge of the heel and inserting your hook into both fabrics at the same time(pic.4). Cut off the thread and weave in the end. The sole with the heel is completed - Pic.5

Arrange the sole with the heel and the second sole, with wrong sides facing each other (pic.6-7).

With **Jeans Blue**, stitch them together by slip stitches inserting your hook through both layers. Start inserting your hook from the sole without the heel. Move around the edge of the sole, avoiding stitching together the area of the heel. Then, cut the thread off, leave a long tail for sewing.

Thread the tail into a tapestry needle and stitch the rest of the sole edges together, inserting the needle through both loops on the sole without the heel and the inner loop of the heel and sew in a running stitch

Use a contrast thread to mark the beginning of each round. Do not remove it until your work is completed

STEP 3. UPPER PART OF THE BOOT (work in continuous round)

Rd 1	**Bright Yellow:** oin the yarn to the middle of the heel (the upper sole without the heel) and work: SC BLO in each st around [40]	 

Rd 2	SC in next 17sts, INC in next st, SC in next 4sts, INC in next st, SC in next 17sts [42] Drop the loop from your hook we will use it later

	Jeans Blue: Work surface slip stitches in between the yellow and **Blue** rounds (the sole and the upper part of the boot). Cut off **Jeans Blue** and weave in	

Rd 3-5	Grab the **Bright Yellow** loop back on your hook and continue working: SC in each st around [42]

Rd 6	SC2tog, SC in next 10sts, SC2tog x9, SC in next 9sts, SC2tog, SC in next st [31]	

Rd 7	SC in next 10sts, SC2tog x6, SC in next 9sts [25]

Rd 8	SC in next 8sts, SC2tog x4, SC in next 9sts [21]	

Rd 9-12	SC in each st around [21]
Rd 13	INC in next st, SC in next 20sts [22]
Rd 14	SC in each st around [22]
Rd 15	SC in next st, INC in next st, SC in each st around [23]
Rd 16	SC in next 2sts, INC in next st, SC in each st around [24]
Rd 17	SC in next 3sts, INC in next st, SC in each st around [25]
Rd 18	SC in next 2sts, INC in next st, SC in each st around [26]
Rd 19-22	SC in each st around [26]
Rd 23	SC in next st, SC2tog, SC in next st, SC2tog, SC in next 20 sts [24]
Rd 24	SC in each st around (pic. 1) [24] Change to **Jeans Blue** in last st. Cut off a thread
Rd 25	**Jeans Blue:** SC BLO in each st around [24] (pic. 2) Cut off a thread and weave in

STEP 4. PULL LOOP

| | **Jeans Blue:** Foundation chain: Chain 14 |
| Rd 1 | 2SC in 2nd st from hook, SC in next 11 sts, 3SC in last st of foundation chain, work in other side of the foundation chain: sl st in each stitch of the foundation chain |

Cut off a thread, weave in. Sew it in place. Imitate a clasp with some **Brown** of **Black** yarn on the outer side of the boot.

STEP 5. EXTERNAL HEEL COUNTER

| Row 1 | **Jeans Blue.** Join the yarn to the third stitch of the rounded heel edge (pic.3) and work: SC BLO in next 5sts [5] |

Row 2-3	Ch1, SC in next 5 sts [5]
Row 4	Ch1, SC2tog, SC in next st, SC2tog [3]/Cut a thread off, leave a long tail for sewing. Attach an external heel counter to the boot. Stuff the bottom of the boot to ensure your crocheted boot stays upright and stable.

TULIP

Rd 1	**Red:** 6SC in magic ring [6] tighten the ring leaving a small opening
Rd 2	INC in each of next 6 sts [12]
Rd 3	*(SC in next st, INC in next st)from*rep x6[18]
Rd 4	*(SC in next st, INC in next st, SC in next st)from*rep x6[24]
Rd 5-12	SC in each st around [24] Cut off **Red** leaving a long tail for sewing

STEM

Grass Green
1. Make a loop on the end of the thread.
2. Insert this loop from the outside in the tulip through the magic ring opening with by a crochet hook.
3. Insert one end of the wooden stick into the magic ring opening.
4. Then insert this end through the loop and tighten the loop. If there is a hot gun, glue it to fix it in place. If you don't have a hot glue, then make a few knots on the stick.
5. Wrap the other tail of the green thread around the wooden stick and fix in place

Stuff the tulip and sew edges together by threading yarn through 4 stitches and tightening the opening as illustrated in the pictures.

LEAF

Grass Green: Chain 20

Row 1 — sl st in 2nd st from hook, sl st in next st, SC in next 2sts, hdc in each stitch across

Cut off a thread

Attach leaves to the stem and fix in place by a glue or wrap a thread around the stem and tighten

LEAF WITH A STICK

1) To begin, grab a wooden stick and measure the length that you would like your leaf to be.

2) (pic.1) Crochet a chain that is equal to the length of the stick.

3) (pic.2)Then single crochet in the second loop from the hook.

4) (pic.3-4)Attach the stick and work single crochet stitches across your chain, carrying the stick inside of stitches as you go.

5) Once you have finished crocheting the leaf, cut the thread and tie a knot at the end of the stick. If necessary, you can cut off any excess from the stick.

6) Finally, hide the end of the stick in the first single crochet stitch.

LARGE LEAF Find a photo tutorial below

	Chain 16 (foundation chain)
Rd 1	sl st in 2nd st from hook, sl st in next 14sts(midrib), on the other side of the chain: SC in next 2 sts, hdc in next st, DC in next st, 2TR in next st, Ch1, sl st in top of prev TR, Ch3, sl st in next st on midrib, SC in next 2 sts, hdc in next st, 2DC in next st, Ch1, sl st in top of last DC, Ch2, sl st in next st on midrib, SC in next 2 sts, hdc in next st, 3DC in last st of the foundation chain, Ch2, sl st in top of last DC of 3DC, (we work on other side of midrib) 3DC BLO in next st, hdc BLO in next st, SC BLO in next 2sts, sl st BLO in next st, Ch4, sl st in 2nd st from hook, 2DC BLO in same st as 4Ch, hdc BLO in next st, SC BLO in next 2 sts, sl st BLO in next st, Ch4, sl st in 2nd st from hook, 2TR BLO in same st as 4Ch, DC BLO in next st, hdc BLO in next st, SC BLO in next 2 sts, sl st in next st

Chain 16 (foundation chain)

sl st in 2nd st from hook, sl st in next 14sts (midrib),

On the other side of the chain: SC in next 2 sts,

hdc in next st,

DC in next st,

2TR in next st,

Ch1,

sl st in next st,

Ch3,

sl st in next st on midrib,

SC in next 2 sts,

hdc in next st,

2DC in next st,

Ch1,

sl st in top of last DC,

Ch2,

sl st in next st on midrib,

SC in next 2 sts,

hdc in next st,

3DC in last st of foundation chain,

Ch2,

sl st in top of last DC

3DC BLO in next st

hdc BLO in next st,

SC BLO in next 2 sts,

sl st BLO in next st,

Ch4,

Large Leaf Pattern

sl st in 2nd st from hook,

2DC BLO in same st as 4Ch,

hdc BLO in next st,

SC BLO in next 2 sts,

sl st BLO in next st

Ch4,

sl st in 2nd st from hook,

2TR BLO in same st as 4Ch

DC BLO in next st,

hdc BLO in next st,

SC BLO in next 2 sts,

sl st in next st

SMALL LEAF Find a photo tutorial below

Chain 10 (foundation chain)

Rd 1 — sl st in 2ⁿᵈ st from hook, sl st in next 8sts(midrib), on the other side of the foundation chain: SC in next 2 sts, hdc in next st, DC in next st, 2TR in next st, Ch1, sl st in top of last TR, Ch3, sl st in same st as 2TR, SC in next 2 sts, hdc in next st, 3DC in last st of the foundation chain, Ch2, sl st in top of last DC of 3DC, (we work on other side of midrib) 3DC BLO in next st, hdc BLO in next st, SC BLO in next 2 sts, sl st BLO in next st, Ch4, sl st in 2ⁿᵈ st from hook, 2DC in same st as 4Ch, hdc BLO in next st, SC BLO in next 2 sts, sl st BLO in next st

Grass Green: Chain 10 (foundation chain)

sl st in 2ⁿᵈ st from hook, sl st in next 8sts (midrib),

On the other side of the chain: SC in next 2 sts,

hdc in next st,

DC in next st,

2TR in next st,

Ch1,

sl st in top of last TR,

Ch3,

sl st in same st as 2TR,

SC in next 2 sts,

hdc in next st,

Small Leaf Pattern

3DC in last st of foundation chain,

Ch2,

sl st in top of last DC of 3DC,

3DC BLO in next,

hdc BLO in next st,

SC BLO in next 2 sts,

sl st BLO in next st,

Ch4,

sl st in 2nd st from hook,

2DC in same st as 4Ch,

hdc BLO in next st,

SC BLO in next 2 sts,

sl st BLO in next st

Result

CROCHET GNOMES

More crochet gnomes patterns, inspiration, social media
Find here

SCAN ME

Made in the USA
Las Vegas, NV
10 July 2023

74452603R00090